YEAST-FREE LIVING

YEAST-FREE LIVING

Annette Annechild
and Laura Johnson

Preface by Charles Kelman, M.D.

A Perigee Book

Important Notice

This book is based on our experiences, and on our studies of nutritional literature. It is not intended, nor should it be regarded, as medical advice. Before changing your diet, it would be prudent to consult with your physician.

Perigee Books
are published by
The Putnam Publishing Group
200 Madison Avenue
New York, NY 10016

Copyright © 1986 by The RGA Publishing Group and
Annette Annechild
All rights reserved. This book, or parts thereof,
may not be reproduced in any form without permission.
Published simultaneously in Canada by
General Publishing Co. Limited, Toronto

Designed by Rhea Braunstein

Library of Congress Cataloging-in-Publication Data

Annechild, Annette.
Yeast-free living.

1. Candidiasis—Diet therapy—Recipes.
2. Candidiasis—Prevention. 3. Yeast-free diet—
Recipes. I. Johnson, Laura. II. Title.
RC123.C3A56   1986   616.9'69   86-18646
ISBN 0-399-51304-3

Printed in the United States of America
5   6   7   8   9   10

Dedicated to the miracle of knowledge which God unfolds, that we may heal ourselves . . .

ACKNOWLEDGMENTS

The authors wish to thank The RGA Publishing Group, especially Jack Artenstein and Angela Hynes; Gene Brissie and Adrienne Ingrum of The Putnam Publishing Group; our recipe testers: Stefni Ritcher and Wende West; Glenn and Louise Latham, Anne and Frank Viscardi, Bill and Inez Johnson, Darrell Johnson, and John Johnson for their love and support; and the doctors whose pioneering research and dedication made this book possible.

Contents

Preface 13

Introduction: What Is Yeast and How Does It Affect You? 15

CHAPTER 1: The Symptoms and Causes of Intestinal Yeast Infection 17

CHAPTER 2: Available Treatments for Intestinal Yeast Infection 27

CHAPTER 3: Vitamin Supplements for Yeast-free Living 33

CHAPTER 4: The Yeast-free Living Diet 37

CHAPTER 5: Recipes for a Yeast-free Breakfast 41

CHAPTER 6: Recipes for a Yeast-free Lunch 51

CHAPTER 7: Recipes for Yeast-free Appetizers and Snacks 71

CHAPTER 8: Recipes for Yeast-free Side Dishes 83

CHAPTER 9: Recipes for Yeast-free Soups 91

CHAPTER 10: Recipes for a Yeast-free Dinner 105

CHAPTER 11: Recipes for Yeast-free Breads and Spreads 133

CHAPTER 12: Recipes for Yeast-free Desserts 145

CHAPTER 13: Maintaining a Yeast-free Lifestyle 153

YEAST-FREE LIVING

Preface

To say that most physicians immediately think of generalized yeast infection when a patient appears with varied and troublesome symptoms would be, to say the least, a gross exaggeration. In fact, most physicians have *never* made that diagnosis in their entire professional careers. To go one step further, any doctor who ascribes headaches, depression, inability to lose weight, high blood pressure and a host of other human sufferings to yeast infections would be labeled by the vast majority of his colleagues as a "quack." There have been other such quacks in medicine. Pasteur, Lister, Curie, Salk and almost every other great contributor has suffered the wrath and scorn of his colleagues before eventually being proven correct.

Healthy skepticism is an important ingredient in scientific endeavor. Skepticism, however, allows for trial, for evaluation, for an open-mindedness that we as physicians do not always have. For a patient who has tried and failed to alleviate his or her suffering, with or without the help of a physician, a trial period on a yeast-free diet, preferably supervised by a physician who is willing to help evaluate the results, seems to be a reasonable approach. In any case, following the diet recommended in this book would certainly seem to be beneficial, since the diet plan follows the principles of what is considered by today's standards to be good nutrition.

Charles D. Kelman, M.D.
Renowned American physician and surgeon
Author of *Through My Eyes* and
Cataracts: What You Must Know About Them

Introduction: What Is Yeast and How Does It Affect You?

Yeasts are single-cell fungi. *Candida albicans* is a family of yeasts that normally live in the body within the intestinal and digestive tract. Frequent use of antibiotics or cortisone, birth-control pills, pregnancy, emotional upset and nutritional deficiencies can cause these yeasts to multiply. It is when these yeasts multiply extensively, or "colonize," that the trouble begins. Flourishing within the digestive tract, they emit toxins that travel throughout the body and weaken the immune system. A weakened immune system renders the body vulnerable to a great variety of ailments and diseases. Frequent headaches, severe depression, lack of energy, recurring viral and fungal infections, allergies, stomach and nervous disorders and increased sensitivity to chemicals are common health problems of a person with a weakened immune system. More serious diseases, such as cancer, multiple sclerosis, psoriasis, arthritis and AIDS, also could develop when the immune system is not functioning normally.

To cleanse the body of excess yeast and to rebuild the immune system, diet is of the utmost importance. On the following pages you will find further information about yeast and yeast-related health problems, as well as about treatments available. Most importantly you will find an exciting, delicious way to eat that will help rid your system of yeast, at the same time helping to rebuild a strong, healthy body. The recipes found in this book use fresh vegetables, whole grains, seafood, poultry and lean meats. These comprise the ideal diet for the rest of your life. Enjoy it and enjoy life!

Annette Annechild
Laura Johnson

ND# 1

The Symptoms and Causes of Intestinal Yeast Infection

The fact that yeast lives in a healthy body makes it difficult to diagnose intestinal yeast infection. Generally, it is diagnosed by studying the patient's *symptoms*, his or her *medical history*, and by the patient's *positive response* to treatments. Immune-system studies are now becoming available that will help confirm the diagnosis of yeast-related health problems. The following is a list of symptoms most often encountered in intestinal yeast infection, these can occur in children, teenagers and adults, both male and female.

1. Frequent headaches, severe depression, lack of energy
2. Recurrent bladder infections, vaginal yeast infection, rectal itching, chronic diarrhea or constipation
3. Menstrual irregularities and severe cramps
4. Frequent fungal infections, such as athlete's foot or jock itch
5. Digestive disorders, including recurring indigestion, heartburn, abdominal pain, bloating and gas
6. Anxiety, mental confusion, lack of coordination, loss of memory, disorientation, insomnia, impotence
7. Muscular weakness, swelling of joints, chest pains, blurred vision
8. Recurrent sore throats, nasal congestion, fluid in ears, persistent cough, rashes or blisters in mouth
9. Symptoms that are aggravated by smoke, perfume, fumes, chemical odors, damp days, moldy places, or by the intake of foods that encourage yeast growth
10. Extreme cravings for sugar, bread or alcoholic beverages
11. Especially in children, colic, recurrent colds and ear infections, hyperactivity
12. Especially in teenagers, depression, nervous-

system disorders, substance abuse, underachievement, erratic behavior

Your medical history is also an important factor in determining the presence of intestinal yeast infection. The following is a list of *causes* for the proliferation of yeast within the system.

1. Frequent or prolonged use of antibiotics*
2. Use of birth-control pills
3. Pregnancy
4. Cortisone or prednisone use
5. Diabetes mellitus
6. Nutritional deficiencies leading to a run-down physical state
7. Severe emotional upset, stress, anxiety

Many factors contribute to the overgrowth of yeast in the intestinal tract. To prevent and/or treat this condition it is important to be aware of your body's intake of food and chemicals, and its reaction to them. Eating foods that are rich in yeast and sugar undoubtedly encourages the growth of yeast within the body. This can produce a second and more advanced stage, in which yeast organisms actually invade the bloodstream through the walls of the intestinal tract. Other substances, such as protein particles that are in the process of being digested can leave the intestinal tract and invade the circulatory system as well. The yeast organisms and other substances then travel throughout your system causing the debilitating symptoms we have just described.

*In his paper titled "*Candida albicans:* An Unsuspected Problem," Jeffrey Bland (Ph.D. nutritional biochemistry) suggests that because of the widespread use of antibiotics in animal feed, which then end up in our meats, we are exposed to long-term, low levels of antibiotics, which greatly increases the risk of yeast infection.

This intestinal yeast invasion may also be the cause of many allergy problems that have been previously impossible to pinpoint as due to any one cause. Depression, mental confusion and emotional problems could be related to this process as well.

Intestinal yeast infection is a relatively "new" ailment, and further research is presently under way. Until the condition is better understood, and more tests are developed for pinpointing it, you may or may not have the immediate support or interest of your family doctor. Our view is that the medical community has often ignored unfamiliar or ground-breaking theories. There are, however, millions of chronically ill people whom the medical community cannot help, and who are therefore diagnosed as "hypochondriacs." The doctors who *do* treat for intestinal yeast infection report a dramatic improvement in these previously untreatable cases.

If you suffer from any the symptoms listed in this chapter, or are someone who seldom feels up to par, before you search out psychiatric help or begin experimenting with medication to fight what ails you, let's take a look at the human body, its anatomy and its reaction to different foods, as they relate to intestinal yeast infection.

THE FOOD MACHINE

Your body is an exquisitely designed piece of machinery. One of its main functions is the digestion of food and elimination of wastes. How well it performs these functions is largely up to you. What and when you feed the machine can greatly influence its performance. A car is a good analogy to the body. The quality of fuel you use in a car directly affects its performance. Keeping the car well maintained and clean also affects performance. A brand-new car, much like a very young body, looks and feels terrific. The effects of bad fuel or bad food are hardly felt because the machine is so new. But in the long run, the care we've taken with the machine becomes the deciding factor in terms of performance and longevity. Being aware of what you put in your machine can make all the difference, both in how you feel today and in the future. Different food groups react differently in the body. In the following pages we will look at each food group, how it is digested and how it affects the body.

SUGARS

The basic fuel of your food machine is glucose; it is vital to the functioning of every cell of the body. All carbohydrates become glucose during the digestive process. White sugar, as we know it, is the combination of glucose and fructose. When this type of sugar enters the body, it encourages yeast growth. Its action in the body is similar to that of the brewer's yeast you bake with: when you put the yeast in warm water it begins to grow, and adding sugar aids the growth, making the yeast very bubbly and active. Table sugar and foods with high quantities of hidden sugar should be avoided as much as possible. Luckily, you can avoid table sugar and still get all the glucose needed to keep your body's cells functioning efficiently. This can be done by eating a wide variety of carbohydrates, which are largely made up of glucose. Granulated sugar is one of the most commonly overeaten foods in our country. Filled with empty calories, it provides an initial rush of energy, but quickly slows the body down. Carbohydrates, however, provide slow-burning fuel to provide long-term energy.

CARBOHYDRATES

The digestion of carbohydrates begins in the mouth. The saliva begins breaking down the disaccharides and polysaccharides, which it then absorbs and converts into glucose. Again, carbohydrates give you long-term energy—be aware: there are no adequate substitutes for carbohydrates. Carbohydrates are the best source for getting enough glucose into your body. Fruit contains a very high concentration of glucose. Wheat, brown rice, millet, barley, oats, corn and legumes are important sources of carbohydrates to incorporate into your diet, as well. They are inexpensive, easy to cook and delicious. Grains also provide fiber, which helps the body eliminate easily. In America the common belief is that carbohydrates make you fat, when actually the opposite is true. Pastries, candy and cake make you fat. Whole grains cleanse the body and keep you fat free. Whole grains, combined with fresh fruits, vegetables and protein, provide the basis for a healthy diet.

PROTEINS

Protein is essential in the diet. It provides our bodies with the needed amino acids to build new tissue and restore damaged tissue. Protein enables your body to replace worn-out cells; build scar tissue to heal wounds; and maintain healthy, beautiful, nails, hair and skin. Protein, however, should not be the mainstay of any diet. With energy being the body's main concern, carbohydrates are essential, too, because protein isn't the best source of glucose. However, if the body was not receiving glucose from any other source, the protein would be converted and supply a sufficient amount of glucose for survival.

The digestion of protein begins in the stomach. It takes the strong acid in the stomach to break apart the protein strands. Water helps this process along. In the buildup of protein, molecules of water are taken out of the amino acids, allowing them to bond together. When water is then added to the amino acids it helps tear them apart and continues the process of digestion. Next the protein moves down to the small intestine for the final stage of digestion. This is the point at which protein particles may enter the bloodstream and contribute to allergies and emotional problems, which a yeast infection could aggravate.

LIPIDS

You may feel that fats are bad for you and absolutely have no place in your daily diet. On the contrary, fats, or lipids, are valuable to the body and are necessary for good health. Fat provides padding for all the body's vital organs, protecting them from outside elements such as temperature fluctuations and hard blows. There are different forms of lipids in the body, triglycerides, phospholipids and sterols. The body stores excess energy in the form of triglycerides. Fatty acids form chains when linked together. Three fatty acids, along with glycerols, are linked to make triglycerides. When each fatty acid in a triglyceride contains a hydrogen atom, it is said to be saturated. When there is a place in the chain where a hydrogen atom is missing, the triglyceride is said to be unsaturated. When there are two or more fatty acids in the chain that are missing hydrogen atoms, the triglyceride is called polyunsaturated. The more saturated a fat, the firmer it is. Some examples would be lard, chicken fat and vegetable oil. Lard is the hardest and the most saturated; chicken fat is semisolid and soft to the touch, less saturated than lard; vegetable oil is almost completely unsaturated and is in liquid form. Oils that come from single sources, such as peanut or corn oil, are the best for your body. At least 2 tablespoons of oil are needed daily to lubricate the system.

The digestion of fat begins in the stomach. Fat separates itself from the other nutrients and is the last to be digested. It forms into large droplets, just as oil separates from water when they are placed together in a bowl. Fat floats to the top of the stomach and waits there until all the other foods have left the stomach. It then travels to the small intestine. An alkaline fluid called bile, secreted by the liver and stored in the gallbladder, is passed into the duodenum, where it attacks the fat droplets. With the help of the digestive muscles the fat droplets are broken down into smaller and smaller droplets. The fat is now ready to be absorbed into the bloodstream. Excess fat not absorbed will be excreted from the body.

DAIRY PRODUCTS

Calcium is a popular concern of today's society, and with good cause. The bones in our bodies are continually changing. The idea that once a bone is formed it is strong and sturdy forever, is false. Calcium is essential for the growth and maintenance of strong bones and teeth. Dairy products, however, do not have to be the body's only source of calcium. Dairy products are believed to be a contributing factor in producing heavy amounts of mucus and saliva in the nose and throat area. If all dairy products are avoided when the body is sick with a cold or flu, it will clear up much more quickly. Vitamin D is necessary for the absorption of calcium across the intestinal cell membranes. It is very important to choose foods that are rich in calcium. Food is an unreliable source for vitamin D. The average adult can acquire the recommended 400 I.U. of vitamin D from exposure to sunlight. Excess amounts of vitamin D are stored in the body and could become toxic. Supplements are rarely needed unless a person is housebound and unable to get outside. Phosphorus, too, plays an important role in the absorption of calcium. When taken at the same time as calcium, both are absorbed more easily. The most readily available source of phosphorus is animal protein. The Recommended Daily Allowance is 800—1200 mg. calcium and phosphorus for adults, the higher levels for pregnant and lactating women. Good sources of calcium are: canned fish with bones, such as sardines; spinach, collard greens, and other dark-green vegetables; and yogurt. Bonemeal is an excellent natural source of phosphorus.

Keeping a daily food diary helps you to monitor your body's reaction to certain foods. This is an example of one such diary.

Daily Food Diary

Date	Time	Food Consumed	How I felt before	How I felt after
6/11	11:30 a.m.	1 med. apple	tired, frustrated	slight stomach pains
6/11	1:00 p.m.	turkey sandwich wheat bread/mayo lettuce	hungry	stomachache subsided feel satisfied

2
Available Treatments for Intestinal Yeast Infection

If after reading the first chapter you recognized in yourself several of the symptoms as well as some of the factors that can cause intestinal yeast infection, the next step is treatment.

There are two ways to approach treatment. The first way is under the direct guidance of your family doctor. We hope he will be aware of the possibilities of intestinal yeast infection and of the prescription drugs that can be taken to speed up yeast elimination. However, since this is a new disease still in the research stage, it is possible your doctor will not be aware of this condition. There is a foundation that has compiled a list of doctors interested in the area of intestinal yeast infection. The foundation's address can be found at the end of this chapter. In addition there are several books, written by doctors, that are available. These are listed in the bibliography at the end of the book.

There also exists a natural and more personal approach to treatment. Next we will discuss the three-point plan for this type of personal treatment. Certainly you should discuss this or any other dietary change with your family physician. But even in the event that you do not have yeast infection, this plan would not be detrimental. Based on natural, healthful, foods and the elimination of environmental yeast, it is a program for well-being that we feel can only serve to benefit both you and your family.

THE THREE-POINT TREATMENT PLAN

1. The first step is the elimination of excess yeast within the body. There are several factors involved in accomplishing this. A yeast-free diet that contains *cleansing foods*, coupled with *vitamin supplements* and *exercise*, is an effective natural approach. A yeast-elimination diet consists of foods that naturally cleanse the body. Especially important are:

AVAILABLE TREATMENTS FOR INTESTINAL YEAST INFECTION

    Garlic
    Onions
    Ginger root
    Cabbage
    Broccoli
    Barley
    Wheat germ
    Olive oil
    Yogurt

At the same time, these foods must be avoided (generally because they contain yeast or feed yeast or may ferment or mold easily):

    Sugar
    Bread and baked goods made with yeast
    Alcoholic beverages
    Vinegar
    Ketchup (and other bottled sauces that are high in sugar)
    Processed meat
    Dried fruit
    Coffee and tea
    Many dairy products
    Fast foods

   Vitamin supplements, which are discussed in detail in Chapter 3, also aid the body in eliminating yeast and in rebuilding the immune system. A multivitamin supplement is recommended, as well as a complete mineral supplement. However, don't count on the supplements as your main source for vitamins and minerals. You must develop a diet that consists of a wide variety of foods; this will help ensure that you are getting all the needed vitamins and minerals, which in turn will make your body feel terrific. The chapters that follow are filled with delicious recipes for preparing all the foods you need.

Exercise contributes to better circulation, digestion and general conditioning. We know that lack of nutrients affects our bodies; so does lack of stimulation. Aerobic exercise conditions the circulatory system, keeping our hearts and our lungs healthy. Through this system, oxygenated blood and nutrients are carried to all of the cells in the body. In order for our cells to work efficiently, each must be given these vital nutrients. It's a cycle that continues, round and round; the cells need certain nutrients, but in order to get these nutrients to the cells we need a strong circulatory system. Exercise and nutrition go hand in hand in keeping our bodies healthy and ready to fight infections.

The elimination of smoke, pollutants and environmental yeast and mold is also of extreme importance. Smoke and pollutants aggravate a yeast condition, and environmental yeast contributes to its intestinal yeast growth. Damp basements, humidifiers, compost, and moldy bathrooms all must be avoided.

2. The second step back to health is the elimination of all immune-suppressive drugs, and antibiotics. Certainly you will need to consult your physician before stopping any medication you are taking under his direction, but if it is at all possible to eliminate drugs in these categories, it will further aid in your treatment of yeast infection.

3. The final and perhaps most important step, in the long run, is your long-term general diet. Not only do you need to eliminate yeast from your system, but you also need to rebuild your body's nutritional support system.

In the next chapter, you will find a discussion of the foods that provide a natural detoxifying effect, as well as help build a strong nutritional base. This diet will not only help you rid yourself of infection, but will also provide you with an excellent food plan for the rest of your life. Fortunately, there is little *deprivation* involved—instead you need to *indulge* yourself with all the wonderful foods nature has provided for your well-being. If you are also interested in shedding a few pounds—this is your chance! This diet will not only please your palate, it will also rid you of *excess fat*. If, however, you happen to be one of the few people in this country who is underweight, this diet will also work for you. When you eat "whole foods," foods that are in their natural nutritional state, and avoid sugar, alcohol and white-flour products, the body eventually assumes its healthy weight and *stays there*.

If your doctor is familiar with intestinal yeast infection, in addition to this three-point personal plan there are also drugs that he can prescribe. Nystatin (sold under the brand names Mycostatin and Nilstat) is the most widely recommended drug for this purpose. It is an antifungal drug that kills yeast and fungi, but does not affect bacteria and other germs. It is available in oral tablets and liquid, vaginal tablets and suppositories, topical powders and internal powders. It is a drug well-tolerated by most people. There are occasionally side effects, which include skin rashes, digestive disorders, headaches, fatigue and general flulike symptoms. These side effects are thought to be the result of the body absorbing a large quantity of dead yeast cells, as it detoxifies. Nystatin is generally prescribed for several months, and in some cases for a year or more.

Ketoconazole, also sold under the brand name Nizoral, is another drug sometimes used. There has been some evidence, however, of allergic reactions and liver irritation. Clotrimazole creams and vaginal tablets have also been found effective in the treatment of oral and vaginal fungal infections, however there is no evidence as to their effectiveness and safety when used for reducing intestinal yeast.

We know that the simple avoidance of sugar, preservatives, fast foods, meat, caffeine, and alcohol generally has a dramatic beneficial effect, and that many of the chronic problems, such as indigestion, fatigue, bloating, headaches, and constipation, disappear with the introduction of a natural, healthful diet.

If your doctor is unaware of intestinal yeast infection, you may want to send a stamped self-addressed envelope to the Price–Pottinger Nutrition Foundation, P.O. Box 2614, La Mesa, CA 92041. This nonprofit foundation has compiled a list of doctors interested in and aware of yeast-related illness.

3

Vitamin Supplements for Yeast-free Living

Whether you decide to take medication to kill the excess yeast in your system or decide to take a more natural approach, you will definitely need extra vitamins and minerals to build your immune system back up. Some people prefer at least to start with a food and vitamin approach, and then, if symptoms continue, to begin treatment with medication. Many foods detoxify the body naturally, and these are used extensively in the recipes in the following chapters. The combination of these foods and supplements may bring on a "detox" reaction for the first few days—flulike symptoms that occur while the body is detoxifying or ridding itself of excess yeast. In the event you do decide to take a drug such as nystatin, we recommend starting the diet two weeks before medication, as this will help moderate any "detox" reactions from the drug.

THE SUPPLEMENT PROGRAM

All supplements are available at your natural-food store or pharmacy; *all must be sugar and yeast free.*

1. A complete multivitamin; high in A, B-1, B-2, B-3, B-5, B-6, B-12, biotin
2. A complete chelated mineral supplement with at least 1000 mg. calcium and 500 mg. magnesium, plus iron, zinc and selenium
3. Vitamin C, at least 1000 mg., time released
4. Propolis, 500 mg. 3 times daily
5. Primrose or linseed oil:
   primrose, 1–2 capsules 2–3 times a day
   linseed, 1–2 tablespoons a day
6. Digestive enzymes (pancreatin) after each meal and at bedtime

VITAMIN SUPPLEMENTS FOR YEAST-FREE LIVING

7. Garlic—odorless capsules, or fresh
8. Amino acids—read labels for dosage
9. Vitamin E, 800 I.U. daily

4
The Yeast-free Living Diet

All of these carefully tested recipes are ideal for the elimination and prevention of yeast colonization in the body. They are delicious, low calorie, easy to prepare and economical besides. It's true that it does take special effort in the beginning to change old eating habits, but press on—*it's worth the effort*. Once you've gotten accustomed to it, food preparation for yourself and your family will be easier than ever before. These recipes are ideal for people of all ages, both with and without yeast-related health problems. They will contribute to your good health and vitality your whole life long.

GENERAL DIETARY GUIDELINES FOR YEAST-FREE LIVING

Foods to enjoy:

Fresh vegetables
Whole grains
Seafood
Poultry
Yogurt
Yeast-free crackers and breads
Beans
Unprocessed nuts
Eggs

Foods to eat in moderation:

Fresh fruits
Meats (except ham, bacon, luncheon meats, sausage or hot dogs—these are to be avoided)

THE YEAST-FREE LIVING DIET

Foods that are especially important in the elimination of yeast and strengthening of the immune system:

Garlic, onions, ginger
Cabbage, broccoli, turnips, kale
Barley, oats, wheat germ, Brazil nuts
Shrimp, scallops, lobster
Yogurt
Olive oil

Foods to avoid:

Sugar, including sucrose, fructose, maltose, lactose, glycogen, glucose, mannitol, sorbitol, balactose, monosaccharides, polysaccharides, honey, molasses, maple syrup and maple sugar, date sugar, brown sugar, raw sugar and turbinado sugar (read labels!)
Yeast and yeast products (again, read all labels!)
Alcoholic beverages
Malt products
Vinegar
Mustard; ketchup; Worcestershire sauce; Accent; MSG; steak, barbecue, chili and soy sauces; pickles; relishes; green olives; sauerkraut
Processed and smoked meats
Dried and candied fruit
Leftovers (freeze instead of refrigerate)
Canned or frozen juices
All coffees and teas
Melons
Mushrooms, morels and truffles
Cheese, milk, sour cream and buttermilk
Tofu
Canned, processed and "fast food"—almost all contain sugar, yeast and/or chemicals

5

Recipes for a Yeast-free Breakfast

Rolled Oat Cereal

Serves 2

1 cup rolled oats
1 tablespoon peanut oil
2¼ cups water
2¼ tablespoons wheat germ
¼ teaspoon cinnamon
⅛ teaspoon nutmeg
½ teaspoon vanilla

Toast oats in oil until they smell sweet, but do not let them brown. Add the water and bring to a boil. Add wheat germ, cinnamon, nutmeg and vanilla. Stir and cover. Simmer 20 minutes over low heat. Serve immediately.

Spiced Oatmeal

Serves 2

2 tablespoons unsweetened apple juice
⅔ cup water
⅓ cup oats
1 apple, cored and finely chopped
¼ cup chopped nuts
1 teaspoon wheat germ
¼ teaspoon ginger
⅛ teaspoon cloves
½ teaspoon cinnamon

Combine all ingredients in a saucepan. Bring to a boil. Reduce heat, and simmer 8–10 minutes. Remove from heat, cover, and let stand 2 minutes. Serve.

Timbale Eggs

Serves 4

1 tablespoon olive oil
1 clove fresh garlic, minced, or 1 teaspoon bottled minced garlic
1 tablespoon finely minced chives
1 small onion, chopped
¼ teaspoon salt
Freshly ground pepper to taste
1 tablespoon minced cilantro
3 tablespoons tomato sauce
¼ teaspoon red pepper
4 large eggs

Preheat oven to 350°F. Heat oil in wok or large skillet. Add garlic, chives and onion. Sauté 2 minutes. Add salt and pepper, cilantro, tomato sauce and red pepper. Stir until well mixed. Remove from heat.

In a separate bowl, beat eggs slightly. Pour sauce in with eggs, and stir until blended. Pour equal portions into individual greased custard cups. Bake in oven for 20–25 minutes, or until set.

Wende West's Best Waffles

Serves 2–4

1 cup raw sesame seeds
1½ cups rolled oats
1½ cups cornmeal
1 teaspoon grated orange rind
1 teaspoon salt
½ teaspoon baking powder
2 tablespoons oil
1 teaspoon vanilla
½ cup fresh-squeezed orange juice
2–3 cups water

Place sesame seeds in a blender with a little water, and blend until almost liquefied. Add oats, and continue to blend. Add remaining ingredients, and blend just until mixed. Cook in a hot waffle iron, and serve with raspberry syrup (recipe follows).

Raspberry Syrup

Yields 1 cup

1 12-ounce bag of frozen unsweetened raspberries*
¼ cup unsweetened apple juice
2 teaspoons cornstarch
½ teaspoon lemon juice

Combine all ingredients in a saucepan, and cook over medium heat until sauce thickens. Serve hot or cold.

*Frozen unsweetened strawberries may be substituted for the raspberries.

Green Pepper Scramble

Serves 2

1 tablespoon olive oil
1 clove fresh garlic, minced, or 1 teaspoon bottled minced garlic
1 small onion, chopped
1 large green pepper, chopped into 2-inch strips
4 eggs, slightly beaten
Salt and pepper to taste
Red pepper flakes to taste (these are hot!)
Salsa (optional)

Heat oil in a wok or large skillet. Add garlic, onion and green pepper; stir fry until pepper is tender. Add eggs, salt and pepper, and red pepper flakes; keep stirring with wooden spoon until eggs reached desired consistency. Serve immediately with salsa, if desired.

Shredded-wheat Egg Puffs

This is a *great* recipe! Not only is it extremely easy to prepare, it's also a uniquely different way to serve eggs. Serve this dish at breakfast or a brunch, and enjoy the compliments that will undoubtedly come your way.

Serves 4

> 2 large biscuits shredded-wheat cereal (with no sugar added)
> 5 large eggs
> ½ large green pepper, chopped
> 2 tablespoons chopped onion
> ¼ teaspoon minced garlic
> 8 dashes Tabasco sauce
> Salt and pepper to taste
> 12 thin avocado slices

Preheat oven to 350°F. Break shredded-wheat biscuits in half, placing each piece into a buttered ovenproof custard cup; crush slightly.

Mix together eggs and all other ingredients, except avocado. Pour egg mixture over wheat biscuits in equal portions. Bake in oven for 20 minutes.

Lay avocado slices over top, and serve immediately.

Asparagus Omelet

Serves 2

4 asparagus spears
4 eggs
1 tomato, chopped
Salt and pepper to taste
2 tablespoons butter
2 tablespoons chopped onion
½ teaspoon minced garlic
2 whole asparagus spears

Steam or boil asparagus for 1 minute until tender crisp. Slice 2 asparagus spears on the diagonal. Leave remaining 2 whole. Beat eggs slightly. Add sliced asparagus, tomato, salt and pepper.

Heat butter in skillet, add onion and garlic, and cook until onion is transparent. Stir in egg mixture, and cook until semisolid. Place whole asparagus spears in the center of omelet, and fold in half. Cover and cook over low heat 1–2 minutes. Serve.

Sunshine Cereal

For a "get-me-going" breakfast, try this one; it will do the trick!

Serves 1–2

1 cup water
½ cup millet
1 tablespoon wheat germ
1 tablespoon bran
1 handful chopped cashews
2 tablespoons plain yogurt
½ sliced banana

Place water and millet in pot. Bring to boil, and simmer uncovered until water is absorbed. Add all other ingredients, except yogurt and banana. Stir well. Serve topped with yogurt and banana. Enjoy!

Asparagus-Stuffed Squash Crêpes

Serves 2–4

Crêpes:

1 small zucchini
½ cup whole-wheat flour
3 eggs, slightly beaten
¼ teaspoon nutmeg
¼ cup water (the water the zucchini is cooked in can be used)

Stuffing:

2 tablespoons margarine
2 eggs
1 bunch baby asparagus, sliced thinly on the diagonal
Salt and freshly ground pepper to taste
Margarine for cooking crêpes

Cut zucchini into chunks, place in a small pot and add just enough water to cover. Bring to a boil, cover, and cook until very tender. Drain liquid, and reserve, if desired. Mash zucchini until smooth. Add flour, the 3 eggs, nutmeg, and ¼ cup of the water. Continue to blend until smooth. Add more liquid, if necessary, to create a thin batter. Set batter aside.

Prepare stuffing by heating the 2 tablespoons margarine in a large skillet. Add the 2 eggs, and scramble; when egg is barely set, add asparagus, salt and pepper; stir fry for 3 minutes, or until asparagus is cooked.

Heat a separate skillet, coat it with margarine. Pour in ⅓ cup batter, tip skillet back and forth to spread batter thin. When little bubbles form around edges of crêpe and batter is set, flip, and cook other side. Keep crêpes warm until all are made.

Place portion of stuffing in each crêpe, and roll up. Drizzle each with melted margarine and sprinkle with nutmeg.

6

Recipes for a Yeast-free Lunch

Basic Brown Rice

There are many types of grains that you can incorporate into your diet—bulgur, millet, rice, rye, oats, wheatberries, amaranth and corn. The general rule of thumb for cooking them is 2 parts liquid to 1 part grain, bring to a boil, cover, and simmer until liquid is absorbed. Bulgur is generally not cooked, however; simply pour boiling water over it and allow to sit until liquid is absorbed.

The following is a foolproof recipe for perfect brown rice. This grain is so cleansing and nutritious that we recommend keeping a pot of it in your refrigerator at all times and eating it often. You'll find it a perfect complement for many of this book's recipes.

Yields about 4 cups

$2^{1}/_{3}$ *cups brown rice*
4 cups water (or soup stock)
1 tablespoon olive oil

Rinse brown rice in cold water. Put water or soup stock in a separate pot and bring to a boil.

Meanwhile, heat oil in a heavy saucepan. Add rice, and sauté over low heat until moisture is absorbed and rice smells nutty. Add the 4 cups boiling water or stock. Allow to boil uncovered for 2–3 mintues. *Do not stir.* Cover, reduce heat to very low, and simmer 45 minutes. *Do not uncover.*

After 45 minutes, remove from heat and allow to sit 15 minutes. Do not remove lid during this time.

VARIATIONS:

Sesame Rice:
In a skillet, over medium heat, toast 2 tablespoons of whole sesame seeds for 3 minutes. Reduce rice amount to 2 cups and add the sesame seeds to the rice before cooking. Cook as usual.

Chestnut Rice:
Cut a slit in the rounded side of each chestnut (6–10 chestnuts). Place in a pot with boiling water, and cook until tender. Remove chestnut meat from shells, and add to rice before cooking. (Canned chestnuts may be used; just chop them up and add to rice before cooking.) Cook rice as usual.

Wheatberry Rice:
Reduce rice amount to 2 cups, and add ⅓ cup wheatberries. Cook as usual.

Shrimp and Brazil Nut Salad

Serves 2

1 pound small shrimp, shelled, cleaned and cooked
1 cup shelled Brazil nuts, chopped
¾ cup plain yogurt
¼ teaspoon garlic powder
¼ teaspoon onion powder
Freshly ground pepper to taste
1 tablespoon chopped fresh cilantro (parsley can be substituted)
Whole romaine lettuce leaves

In large bowl, mix shrimp, nuts, yogurt, spices and cilantro together. Place in refrigerator, and chill thoroughly. Serve cold on top of whole romaine lettuce leaves.

Best Egg Salad Ever

Serves 4

6 hard-boiled eggs
1 stalk celery, finely diced
1 scallion, finely chopped
2 teaspoons sesame seeds
¼ cup mayonnaise, or to taste (see recipe page 82)
Freshly ground pepper and salt to taste

Combine all ingredients and chill thoroughly. Serve with your favorite yeast-free bread or cracker. This is also good served on a bed of lettuce garnished with crisp raw vegetables.

Fresh Beet and Carrot Salad

Serves 4

8 fresh beets (with tops)
8 fresh carrots
1½ tablespoons olive oil
1 teaspoon lemon juice
1 teaspoon basil
1 teaspoon oregano
1 tablespoon finely chopped beet leaves from tops
3 hard-boiled eggs, chopped
1 tablespoon sesame seeds

Wash beets. Trim bottom of each bulb and cut stems 4 inches from beet bulb top. Mince beet leaves and reserve. Place beets and carrots on steamer rack in pot, and steam 20–40 minutes, or until tender when pierced with a fork. Rinse with cold water, peel beets and let cool. (If beets are large they will require more cooking time than the carrots.)

In large bowl, combine oil, lemon juice, basil, oregano and chopped beet leaves. Reserve. When beets and carrots are cool, dice by hand, or shred in food processor. Add beets, carrots, chopped egg, and sesame seeds to the bowl with the oil. Toss until oil is absorbed and everything is coated. Serve at room temperature, or chilled.

Tangy Lobster Salad

Serves 4

2 tablespoons olive oil
½ teaspoon cumin seed
¼ teaspoon sage
¼ teaspoon cayenne pepper
10 ounces shredded cooked lobster meat, fresh, canned or frozen
Variety of lettuce: romaine, arugula, radicchio
1 small red onion, sliced

In a bowl, mix together the oil, cumin, sage and cayenne. Add lobster meat, and marinate in oil sauce while preparing lettuce leaves.

Wash and tear lettuce leaves into small bite-sized pieces. Add onion. Toss lettuce with lobster and oil until every piece is coated with sauce. Chill thoroughly, and serve with yeast-free crackers or rice cakes.

Warm Chicken Salad

Serves 4

1 pound chicken (warmed up leftover chicken also works well with this recipe)
Spring water for cooking
1 bay leaf
2 cloves garlic
1 cup fresh pineapple chunks
1 cup seedless grapes
1 small head romaine lettuce
1 small bunch arugula (Italian lettuce—if you can find it)

1 tablespoon olive oil
1 teaspoon sweet thyme
1 teaspoon lemon juice

Place raw chicken pieces in a large pot, cover with water, add bay leaf and garlic, and bring to a boil. Reduce heat and continue to cook 35–40 minutes, or until chicken is done. Remove chicken from pot, set aside until cool enough to handle. (Reserve cooking liquid. Refrigerate overnight. Then skim off fat, and refrigerate or freeze liquid for use later as soup stock.)

Combine pineapple chunks and grapes together in a large bowl. Tear lettuce leaves into bite-sized pieces and add to fruit. When chicken is cool enough to handle, remove skin and discard. Remove meat from bones, and cut into bite-sized pieces. Toss chicken with lettuce and fruit, drizzle with oil, and sprinkle with thyme and lemon juice; toss until well coated. Serve warm.

Spicy Hot Black Beans

Serves 6

1 12-ounce package black beans (try this with other kinds of beans as well)
Spring water for soaking and cooking
2 cloves fresh garlic, minced, or 1 teaspoon bottled minced garlic
2 teaspoons fresh parsley, minced
1–2 teaspoons curry powder
½ teaspoon cayenne pepper (or to taste—it's hot)

Soak black beans in spring water overnight.

Drain beans. Place in a large skillet along with fresh spring water. Bring to a boil, reduce heat, and add garlic and parsley. Cover, and simmer 1½ hours. Check the water level occasionally, adding more as needed. When beans are tender, uncover and add spices. Cook uncovered until water has evaporated and the beans reach the desired consistency. Serve hot.

This is delicious mixed with brown rice. This recipe also freezes well.

Crab and Potato Salad

Serves 4

6 red (new) potatoes
2 scallions, finely chopped
3 hard-boiled eggs, chopped
8 ounces crab meat, fresh, canned or frozen
2 tablespoons mayonnaise, or to taste (see recipe page 82)
2 dashes Tabasco sauce
1 tablespoon minced fresh parsley
1 stalk celery, finely diced
1 tablespoon linseed oil
½ teaspoon freshly ground pepper
1 tablespoon lemon juice

Wash potatoes, leaving skins on, and place in boiling water. Cook 10–15 minutes, or until tender when pierced with a fork. Do not overcook; they will get mushy.

When potatoes are done, dice into small chunks and place in a large bowl. Add remaining ingredients, and stir until well blended. Chill thoroughly and serve.

Two Tasty Toppings for Matzo Bread

Serves 2

1 ripe avocado
½ teaspoon garlic powder
Dash Tabasco sauce
1 jalapeño pepper, finely minced
Matzo bread

Mash avocado in a small bowl. Add remaining ingredients, and stir until mixed. Serve spread on matzo bread, or use as a dip for the bread.

Serves 2

Matzo bread
1 can tuna, drained
2 tablespoons mayonnaise (see recipe page 82)
1 teaspoon paprika
1 cucumber, sliced
2 tomatoes, sliced

Preheat broiler. Break matzo bread into large pieces; set aside. Mix tuna, mayonnaise and paprika together. Spread tuna over matzo pieces. Layer each piece with cucumber and tomato slices. Broil 3 minutes. Serve hot.

Shredded Carrot Salad

Serves 4

½ *pound raw cashews*
1 pound carrots, shredded
¼ *cup plain yogurt*
2 teaspoons olive oil
1 teaspoon lemon juice
Freshly ground pepper to taste

Place cashews in a small pan, cover with water and simmer 10 minutes. Drain well. Meanwhile, combine remaining ingredients and stir until well mixed. Add cashews, and toss with carrot mixture. Chill thoroughly.

Anytime Rice Cake Snacks

Serves 4

2 ripe avocados, sliced
4 rice cakes
1 tomato, sliced
Juice of ½ fresh lemon
Salt and pepper to taste

Place avocado slices onto rice cakes; smash gently. Top with tomato slices, squeeze on lemon juice, add salt and pepper—now enjoy!

Tabbouleh Salad

Serves 4

2 cups cracked wheat bulgur
4 cups boiling water
⅓ cup linseed oil
⅓ cup fresh-squeezed lemon juice
Salt and pepper to taste
½ cup chopped cilantro (optional)
½ cup chopped fresh parsley
½ bunch fresh dill picked from stems (optional)
¼ cup minced scallions
2 large tomatoes, diced
½ cup celery, diced
1 cucumber, diced

Pour boiling water over cracked wheat in bowl, set aside and let stand 1 hour. Meanwhile, prepare all other ingredients. When liquid is absorbed, grain is ready; add remaining ingredients, mix well. Refrigerate until completely chilled, and serve cold.

Variation: Try adding these vegetables, or your own favorites:
   ¼ cup cooked beets, diced
   ½ cup cooked cauliflower, diced
   ½ cup cooked brussels sprouts, quartered

Chili con Carne

This is great for a *chilly* night. Make it as spicy as you want by varying the amount of chili powder and peppers—the hotter it is the better (that's our opinion, though some would beg to differ with that).

Serves 6

> 1 pound lean ground beef
> ½ onion, chopped
> 16 ounces kidney beans (soaked overnight in water to cover beans completely, and drained)
> 4 tomatoes, diced
> 3½ teaspoons chili powder
> 1 teaspoon oregano
> ½ teaspoon ground cumin
> Salt and pepper to taste
> 1 8-ounce can tomato sauce (read label!), or 1 cup homemade (see page 127)
> 1 cup water
> 1–2 jalapeño peppers, chopped (optional—it'll make it hot!)

Brown beef in skillet, add onion. Drain off fat when meat is completely cooked. Add beans, all but 2½ cups,* tomatoes, spices, sauce, water, and chopped jalapeños, if desired. Simmer 45 minutes, or until chili is desired consistency.

---

*Extra beans can be used for Kidney Bean Salad (page 66).

The Best Homemade Refried Beans and Tortillas

Don't rule out Mexican food just because you're cutting cheese products from your diet. With refried beans like these you'll never miss the cheese.

Tortillas made from scratch are delicious as well as easy. Recipes follow for both corn and whole-wheat flour tortillas. They freeze well, so make up a bunch at a time!

Serves 4

Refried beans:
>*1 pound dried pinto beans*
>*Spring water for soaking and cooking beans*
>*1 cup butter or margarine*
>*Salt to taste*

Wash and drain beans. Place in dish, cover with spring water, and soak overnight.

Drain the spring water from beans, and place them in a 3-quart pan. Add enough fresh spring water to cover beans. Bring to a boil. Reduce heat, cover, and cook at a low boil until beans mash readily (about 3 hours).

Drain off the water, add butter to the beans, and mash until smooth and the butter is absorbed. Add salt to taste. Serve hot or reheat.

Yields 12

Corn Tortilla:
>*2 cups masa harina (dehydrated cornmeal flour—found in most grocery stores)*
>*1¼ cups warm water*

Mix flour with water; if more water is needed to hold dough together, add 1 tablespoon at a time until dough is easy to shape into a smooth ball. Divide dough into 12 equal parts. Carefully roll each ball into a 6-inch circle.

Place each tortilla onto a preheated, ungreased griddle over medium heat. Cook for approximately 2 minutes, turning frequently, until tortilla looks dry and is lightly browned. Serve immediately. Cool leftover tortillas, wrap tightly or place in an airtight container, and freeze.

Yields 12

Whole-wheat Flour Tortilla:
 3 cups whole-wheat flour
 2 teaspoons baking powder
 ½ teaspoon salt
 ¾ cup water

Stir dry ingredients together. Slowly add water—just enough to form a crumbly dough (similar to pie-crust dough). Mold it with your hands until it holds together, adding more water 1 tablespoon at a time if needed. Divide dough into 12 equal parts. Carefully roll each ball into a 9-inch circle.

Place each tortilla on an ungreased griddle, preheated to 375°F. Turn and cook until golden brown. If tortillas stick, lower heat. Tortillas may puff up—place your spatula on top of the tortilla and press gently, this will allow the tortilla to cook evenly. Cool leftover tortillas, and freeze in an airtight container.

Toppings and fillings for both corn and flour burritos: avocado, tomato, onion, hot peppers, salsa, lettuce, bell pepper, shredded chicken, hamburger, shredded beef

Kidney Bean Salad

Serves 4

2½ cups kidney beans, which have been soaked overnight*
3 cups water
1 cup fresh peas
1 small can garbanzo beans
¼ cup chopped almonds
½ cup finely chopped broccoli
3 tablespoons plain yogurt

Place beans and water into a 2-quart pot, bring to a boil, and cook 1 hour, or until beans are tender. Drain and place in refrigerator to cool. Meanwhile, place peas, garbanzo beans, almonds and broccoli in a large bowl.

When beans are cool, add to the pea mixture. Add yogurt and stir well. Refrigerate for at least 4 hours, preferably overnight. Serve cold.

---

*See recipe for Chili con Carne (page 63).

RECIPES FOR A YEAST-FREE LUNCH

Chicken-Stuffed Chili Peppers

Serves 4

8 5-inch chili peppers
2 large boneless chicken breasts
1 tablespoon olive oil
2 cloves fresh garlic, minced, or 2 teaspoons bottled minced garlic
Freshly ground pepper to taste
½ cup tomato sauce
Red pepper to taste

Preheat oven to 350°F. Cut off the tops of each chili pepper. Carefully remove the seeds and membrane from inside. Set peppers aside. Cut each chicken breast into 4 long strips. Heat oil in a wok or large skillet. Add garlic, chicken strips, pepper, tomato sauce, and red pepper; sauté 3–5 minutes, or until chicken is fully cooked. Slip one chicken strip into each chili pepper, along with a small amount of sauce. Place in a baking dish, and pour remaining sauce over the top. Cover with foil. Bake in oven for 10 minutes, or until peppers are heated through.

Conchiglie Pasta with Fried Zucchini

Serves 4

1 pound package conchiglie (seashell-shaped pasta)
2 small zucchini
1 onion
1 tablespoon olive oil
1 clove fresh garlic, minced, or 1 teaspoon bottled minced garlic

Prepare conchiglie as directed on package. Drain well. Meanwhile, prepare zucchini by slicing into thin circles. Prepare onion by chopping into 2-inch pieces, or smaller. Heat oil in wok or large skillet. Add garlic, onion and zucchini; stir fry 5–7 minutes, or until zucchini is golden. Pour over cooked pasta, toss and serve immediately.

Latham's Lobster-Stuffed Avocado

Serves 4

10 ounces lobster meat, fresh, frozen or canned
2 cups cooked elbow macaroni, well drained
½ cup fresh peas
½ cup mayonnaise (see recipe page 82)
½ teaspoon rosemary
¼ teaspoon salt
1 teaspoon lemon juice
2 large ripe avocados, peeled and cut in half
½ teaspoon freshly ground pepper
2 lemons, quartered

In a large bowl, combine lobster, macaroni and peas. Stir in mayonnaise, rosemary, salt and lemon juice. Stir to mix well. Scoop equal portions of lobster stuffing into each avocado half. Top with fresh pepper. Serve with lemon wedges.

7

Recipes for Yeast-free Appetizers and Snacks

Sizzling Scallops

Serves 4

1 pound cleaned fresh sea scallops (they are the larger scallops), or 1-inch chunks of shark or swordfish
⅛ cup powdered walnuts* (optional)
¾ cup wheat germ
¼ cup bran flakes
3 eggs
1 cup peanut oil for cooking

Rinse scallops with cool water. Pat dry. Mix nut powder, wheat germ and bran flakes together. Place on flat plate. Beat eggs in small bowl. Set bowl close to plate. Put peanut oil in wok or deep frying pan over medium heat. Dip scallops into egg, roll in the nut mixture, then drop carefully into hot oil. Fry until golden. Adjust the heat so as not to burn the scallops, but to brown them lightly. Scallops should only take 2–3 minutes to cook. Test by cutting into one: if it flakes easily with a fork and is a white color, it's ready to be eaten.

---

*To powder walnuts, place nuts in a food processor and grind until finely powdered.

RECIPES FOR YEAST-FREE APPETIZERS AND SNACKS

Beet Boats

Yields 16

8 small beets
10 ounces crab meat, canned or fresh
2 teaspoons minced fresh parsley
1 teaspoon lemon juice

Wash beets, remove stems 4 inches above bulbs. (Reserve beet greens for later use.)* Place beets on a steamer rack, and steam 20–40 minutes, or until tender when pierced with fork (larger beets take longer). Remove from heat and rinse well with cold water. Peel and let cool. Meanwhile, mix together crab meat, parsley and lemon juice.

When beets are cool, halve, and scoop out centers with melon baller or teaspoon, making a hollow. Stuff with crab mixture. Serve as an appetizer, or for lunch along with stir-fried beet greens.

*Fresh beet greens can be cooked exactly like spinach. Simply remove any thick stems and discard, then either steam or stir fry leaves. Delicious seasoned with lemon juice.

Sweet Potato Squash Cakes

These appetizers are so delicious you might try them for lunch.

Yields about 12

2 large sweet potatoes
1 small crookneck squash
1 cup whole-wheat flour
1 teaspoon baking powder
1/8 teaspoon pepper
1/2 teaspoon basil
1/2 teaspoon garlic powder
4 cups peanut oil for cooking
Lemon wedges

Cut sweet potatoes and squash into small chunks. Place on a steamer rack over boiling water, cover, and steam 10–15 minutes, or until tender. The squash may be done before the potatoes; remove each when tender. Mash cooked potatoes and squash together. Stir in flour and baking powder. Add seasonings, and mix until blended. Form into balls.

Heat oil in a wok or deep frying pan. Using a slotted spoon, carefully drop balls into the hot oil; lift out when golden. Drain on paper towels. Serve warm with fresh lemon wedges.

RECIPES FOR YEAST-FREE APPETIZERS AND SNACKS

Poached Scallops

For an appetizer the scallops will be placed on a toothpick, but this dish is delicious enough to be a main course.

Serves 8 as appetizer
4 as entrée

> 3 cups bay scallops
> Water
> 1 bay leaf
> 2 sprigs cilantro
> 2 tablespoons butter
> Fresh-squeezed lemon juice to taste
> Lemon wedges

Poach scallops in enough water to cover them. Add the bay leaf and cilantro. Poach 3–5 minutes. After poaching, drain off water and remove herbs. Stir in butter to coat scallops, and sprinkle with lemon juice. Slip 1–2 scallops onto a toothpick, and place on platter garnished with lemon wedges. Serve warm.

Vegetable Pâté

Yields 1 loaf

2 cups cooked and mashed lentils
2 cups crumbled stale yeast-free bread or crackers
2 cups water (for soaking bread or crackers)
1 tablespoon linseed oil
2 onions, chopped
½ teaspoon thyme
½ teaspoon coriander
½ teaspoon basil
1 teaspoon salt, or to taste
½ teaspoon pepper
3 tablespoons minced fresh parsley
1 tablespoon miso
1 tablespoon margarine

Soak crumbled bread or crackers in water at least 1 hour. Preheat oven to 350°F. Heat oil in a wok or large skillet. Add onions and sauté 2–3 minutes. Add soaked bread, and continue to cook 15 minutes, stirring occasionally. Add thyme, coriander, basil, salt, pepper, lentils, miso and margarine. Cook an additional 5 minutes. Pour mixture into a greased mold or loaf pan, and bake in oven for 30 minutes. Chill overnight.

Slip out of mold and serve with your favorite yeast-free cracker.

Rice Balls

Yields 15

1 teaspoon salt
1 cup cold water
2 cups cooked brown rice (see page 52)
A variety of coatings:
  sesame seeds
  finely chopped nuts
  wheat germ
  cooked, mashed aduki beans
Peanut oil for deep frying (optional)

Mix salt and water together in a small bowl. Dip fingers into water; this will help prevent the rice from sticking to you. Shape 2 teaspoons of cooked rice into a ball. Repeat until all rice is used. Roll balls in different coatings and serve warm or cold.

If deep frying rice balls, fill a wok or deep-fryer ⅔ full with peanut oil. Drop rice balls into hot oil, and cook until golden.

Sesame Chicken Rolls

Yields 30–40

4 boneless chicken breasts
1 tablespoon margarine
¼ teaspoon paprika
¼ teaspoon garlic powder
½ cup sesame seeds

Remove skin from chicken breasts and discard. Slice chicken into 2-inch chunks. Heat margarine in a wok or large skillet. Add chicken pieces, paprika and garlic powder. Stir fry 7–10 minutes, or until chicken is fully cooked. Remove chicken from heat, and slip each piece onto a toothpick. Roll chicken in sesame seeds and serve as an appetizer, warm or cold.

Variation: Instead of rolling chicken in sesame seeds, wrap each piece of cooked chicken with a snow-pea pod before slipping it onto toothpick.

RECIPES FOR YEAST-FREE APPETIZERS AND SNACKS

Crab Balls

Yields 16

8 ounces crab meat, fresh, canned or frozen
¼ cup whole-wheat flour
⅛ cup wheat germ
½ teaspoon baking powder
½ teaspoon garlic powder
Freshly ground pepper to taste
1 egg, slightly beaten
1 tablespoon minced fresh parsley
¼ cup plain yogurt
4 cups peanut oil for deep frying
Lemon wedges

Combine all ingredients, except peanut oil and lemon wedges. Mix thoroughly. Form mixture into small balls. Heat oil in a wok or deep frying pan. Drop crab balls into hot oil, and cook until golden on all sides. Serve hot with yogurt sauce (recipe follows) and lemon wedges.

Yogurt sauce:
Combine ½ cup plain yogurt, 1 teaspoon paprika, 1 teaspoon lemon juice, 1 teaspoon finely minced parsley.

Zucchini Chips

Serves 2

2 small zucchini
Vegetable salt substitute (check label for MSG—avoid it!)

Preheat broiler. Slice zucchini into paper-thin circles. Place on lightly greased cookie sheet. Sprinkle sparingly with vegetable salt. Place in the broiler 1½ minutes; flip over, and boil for another 1 minute or so, until crisp and golden.

Maria's Perfect Guacamole

Serves 4–6

4 medium ripe avocados
1 medium tomato
1 small onion
1 small green hot chili
Juice of ½ lemon
Salt to taste

Peel skin from avocados and remove pits. Mash avocados in a large bowl until smooth. Mince tomato, onion and chili; mix together. Add mixture, along with lemon juice, to mashed avocados, and blend well with a fork. Add salt to taste. Serve at room temperature, or chilled.

Tahini Vegetable Dip

Yields 1 cup

1 cup sesame paste (also called tahini—can be found in natural-food stores)
3 teaspoons minced garlic, bottled or fresh
1½ tablespoons lemon juice
Olive oil

In a blender, combine all ingredients, except the olive oil. Slowly add the oil until the desired dipping consistency is reached. Chill thoroughly and serve with a variety of different vegetables.

Banana Dip

This dip is delicious with raw vegetables or spread on yeast-free crackers.

Yields 2–3 cups

3 ripe bananas
1 cup plain yogurt
2 teaspoons finely minced onion
Salt to taste

Mash bananas in a large bowl. Stir in remaining ingredients until well blended. Chill thoroughly.

Easy Mayonnaise

Yields 1½ cups

1 whole egg plus 1 egg yolk
½ tablespoon lemon juice
½ teaspoon white pepper
1 cup safflower oil
½ cup peanut oil

In blender or food processor, blend egg, egg yolk, lemon juice and white pepper together until well blended. With blender still running, slowly pour in oils. Store in refrigerator in a tightly covered plastic container.

8
Recipes for Yeast-free Side Dishes

Garlic Steamed Artichokes with Jim and Barbara Parker's Lemon Dipping Butter

Serves 4

> 4 artichokes
> 2 cloves garlic
> 4 tablespoons olive oil
> 1 teaspoon rosemary

Dip
> *Juice of 2 lemons stirred into 6 tablespoons melted butter (or try substituting lime juice for the lemon juice; it's very good)*

Wash artichokes and clip the tips off the ends of the leaves. Cut off stems to provide a base on which artichokes can sit upright. Place artichokes in a large pot with ¼ inch of water. Peel the garlic cloves and separate into sections. Place the garlic throughout the artichoke leaves. Mix oil and rosemary together, and pour over artichokes, coating as many of the leaves as possible. Cover pot securely and bring water to a boil. Steam artichokes 45–60 minutes, depending on size. Check the water level periodically; add more as needed. Remove garlic and serve artichokes hot with dip.

Variation: Instead of lemon or lime dipping butter, when you remove the garlic from the artichokes mash it into 6 tablespoons softened or melted butter. This is an excellent dip, and it tastes great spread on yeast-free bread as well.

Tarragon Beets

Serves 2–4

6 fresh beets
1 tablespoon olive oil
1 teaspoon tarragon
½ teaspoon lemon juice
½ teaspoon sesame seeds

Wash beets, remove stems 4 inches above beet bulbs. Place beets onto a steamer rack over boiling water, cover, and steam 20–40 minutes, or until tender. Meanwhile, mix together remaining ingredients, except sesame seeds. Set aside.

When beets are tender when pierced with a fork, remove from steamer rack, peel, slice and place on serving platter. Drizzle with dressing. Sprinkle with seeds. Serve warm or cold.

Dick and Janice Haworth's Caraway Cabbage

Serves 4

1 head cabbage
2 tablespoons olive oil
1 teaspoon minced garlic
1½ tablespoons caraway seeds
Salt and pepper to taste

Shred cabbage, or chop into small pieces. Heat oil in a wok or large skillet, add garlic, and stir fry 1 minute. Add cabbage, caraway seeds, salt and pepper. Sauté 3 minutes, or until cabbage is tender crisp. (Do not overcook cabbage—this spoils the delicate texture.)

Red Ginger Cabbage Sauté

Serves 2 as entrée
4 as side dish

1 medium head red cabbage
2 tablespoons peanut oil
1 teaspoon minced fresh ginger root
1 small onion, finely chopped
1 teaspoon sesame seeds (unhulled)
Salt and freshly ground pepper to taste (try cayenne pepper if you like it really hot)
¼ cup walnut halves or pieces

Wash cabbage, and cut into small wedges. Heat oil in wok or large frying pan; add ginger, onion, sesame seeds. Stir fry 2 minutes. Add cabbage, salt and pepper, and walnuts; toss. Continue to cook until cabbage is tender crisp. Serve hot, alone or over brown rice.

Variation: Serve for lunch cold, with a splash of fresh-squeezed lemon juice.

Fresh Minted Cauliflower and Peas

Serves 2

1 cup fresh cauliflower flowerets
1 cup fresh peas
1 tablespoon margarine, melted
1 teaspoon finely chopped fresh parsley
1 teaspoon finely chopped fresh mint
Freshly ground pepper to taste

Place cauliflower and peas on a steamer rack (the basket-type steamer works best for this recipe) over boiling water, and cook, covered, for 3–5 minutes, or until vegetables are tender crisp. Mix melted margarine, parsley and mint together in bottom of a large serving dish. Remove vegetables from steamer, and add to serving dish. Toss vegetables to coat. Season to taste. Serve immediately.

Steamed Garlic Brussels Sprouts

Serves 4

1 pound brussels sprouts
4 cloves fresh garlic, minced, or 2 teaspoons bottled minced garlic
2 tablespoons olive oil
Lemon wedges

Wash brussels sprouts. Slice off bottoms and make a small X in each. Place in a heatproof dish. Mix garlic and olive oil together, and pour over sprouts. Place sprouts on a steamer rack over boiling water, cover, and steam 10–15 minutes, or until tender. Serve hot with lemon wedges.

Squash Medley

Serves 2

1 small zucchini
1 small crookneck squash
½ small acorn squash
½ small butternut squash
Vegetable salt substitute (check labels for MSG)
Freshly ground pepper to taste

Preheat broiler. Cut all squash into bite-sized chunks. Place onto a steamer rack in a large pot, and steam 5–7 minutes, or until tender when pierced with a fork.

Remove squash from steamer and place on a baking sheet. Sprinkle with vegetable salt and pepper. Place in broiler, and cook 2–3 minutes to crisp. Remove to serving platter. Delicious served with brown rice.

Raw Vegetable Salad

Serves 4–6

1 head cabbage, shredded
1 pound carrots, shredded
1 small onion, diced
2 tablespoons lemon juice
¼ teaspoon freshly ground pepper
6 ounces plain yogurt
½ teaspoon cumin seeds

Combine all ingredients. Chill thoroughly and serve.

Variation: Add shredded raw beets!

Hot Walnut Shredded Carrots

Serves 4

½ cup walnuts, finely chopped
1½ cups water
1 pound carrots, shredded
1 large scallion, finely minced
1 teaspoon ginger root, finely minced
1 tablespoon butter
¼ teaspoon ground coriander
1½ tablespoons fresh-squeezed lemon juice
Salt and pepper to taste

Preheat oven to 350° F. In a shallow pan, spread walnuts in a single layer, and toast in oven 5 minutes. Set aside. In a large saucepan, bring the water to a boil over high heat. Add carrots, reduce heat, cover, and cook until tender, about 5 minutes. Drain and set aside.

In another saucepan, combine scallion, ginger, butter and coriander. Sauté over medium heat for 1 minute. Add carrots, lemon juice, salt and pepper; stir, and heat through. Serve hot, garnished with toasted walnuts.

Peter Robert's Golden Potato Pockets

Fresh corn cut from the cob—there's not much that can match that delicious flavor. This recipe takes advantage of that fact to turn a plain potato into a feast.

Serves 4

- 4 baking potatoes
- 4 ears fresh corn
- 3 tablespoons minced turnip
- Salt and pepper to taste
- 3 tablespoons butter or margarine

Preheat oven to 400° F. With a fork, puncture each potato; wrap in foil. Bake in oven for about 2 hours, or until tender. Meanwhile, place ears of corn in boiling water, and cook 3–5 minutes; let cool.

When potatoes are done, preheat oven to 350° F. Place the minced turnip, salt, pepper and butter into a small dish, and mix well. Cut corn from cob and mix into butter mixture. Slice the top off each potato, leaving the potato whole, and hollow out to form a pocket. Place an equal portion of the corn mixture into each potato. Put stuffed potatoes onto a baking dish, place in oven. Heat through and serve.

9

Recipes for Yeast-free Soups

YEAST-FREE LIVING

Vegetarian Garbage Bag Stock

Keeping a plastic garbage bag in your refrigerator is the first step to having a delicious soup stock on hand. It's easy and economical. Simply save:

Any and all vegetable peelings or trimmings (wash all vegetables before peeling) Our favorites for the most flavor are:

> Potato (peels only)
> Carrot (tops can be added too)
> Onion (also the root end that usually gets tossed out)
> Tomato
> Cucumber
> Ginger (not too much or it will impart too strong a flavor; but the peelings from 2–3 inches of fresh ginger root will give an elusive flavor to a batch of broth)
> Garlic (all the skins as well as leftover cloves)
> Tough or wilted outer leaves of cabbage or lettuce
> Parsley (stems and wilted leaves)
> The tough strings from large celery stalks plus trimmings from tops and bottoms of stalks
> Eggshells—yes, eggshells!—well rinsed

Add anything vegetarian you wish to the garbage bag. If you're doubtful about the flavor—strength, bitterness, etc.—taste a bit of what you're adding. If the flavor is extremely strong, use your own judgement as to how much of that particular flavor you want in the finished stock. If you end up adding too much of one thing—for instance, ginger peel—you haven't ruined your stock. Simply add another cup of water, and taste again. If it is still too strong, cut up 1 small onion and 1 small carrot, add these to the stock, and simmer for another 20–30 minutes.

To make stock: Place equal parts "garbage" and water, cup for cup, in a large pot. Simmer, covered, 45 minutes to 1 hour. Strain, cool, and refrigerate or freeze until wanted.

This stock can be used for all soup bases, though you still will need to add seasonings. It can replace water for sauces and even for rice making—it's vitamin packed and tasty as can be.

If you prefer a meat- or fish-based stock, simply save beef or chicken bones, or heads and tails of fish. Boil several hours, then strain and refrigerate.

Grandma's Lentil Soup

Serves 4

1 cup lentils
6 cups water
1 teaspoon salt
1 stalk celery, chopped
3 carrots, chopped
2 onions, diced
2 tablespoons linseed oil

Rinse lentils with cold water. Place the 6 cups water, the salt and lentils into a soup pot, and bring to boiling. Lower heat, cover, and simmer 30 minutes. Meanwhile, wash and slice vegetables. In a skillet, heat 2 tablespoons oil. Add celery, carrots and onions, and stir fry 5–7 minutes. Add vegetables to soup pot, and simmer 15 minutes. Serve.

Christmas Soup

Don't wait till next Christmas to try it! This soup gets its name from the beautiful red and green color the tomatoes and peppers lend. It is a perfect soup indeed, for holiday dinners, but is also an ideal way to use up those fat, soft, garden tomatoes in summer. In winter we use canned tomatoes; it's not quite the same, but it sure is good. Either way, one bowlful is a delicious light meal in itself. The soup will keep for days in your refrigerator.

Serves 4–6

> 3 large onions, chopped
> 2 green bell peppers, chopped
> 4 tablespoons olive oil
> 1 tablespoon flour
> 5 cups vegetable stock or spring water
> 1 bay leaf
> ½ teaspoon oregano
> 1 teaspoon basil
> ½ teaspoon red pepper (or to taste—it's hot)
> 4 tablespoons chopped fresh parsley
> ½ cup pearl barley
> 1½ pounds fresh tomatoes, peeled* and chopped, or canned tomatoes (if using canned, check label for sugar)
> **Freshly ground black pepper**
> **Grated Parmesan cheese (optional)**

Chop the onions and the bell peppers; sauté them in the olive oil in your soup pot, over medium heat for 3 minutes.

---

*To peel fresh tomatoes, carefully drop into boiling water for 1 minute; lift out. The skin will peel off easily. Chop and set aside. If canned, lift out whole tomatoes and chop. Add with packing water along with the tomatoes.

Stir in the flour and continue to cook for 3 minutes. Add the remaining ingredients except the black pepper and cheese. Bring to a boil, cover, reduce heat, and simmer 2 hours. Serve hot with fresh black pepper. When you're on the maintenance program, a sprinkling of Parmesan cheese is the most delicious "snow."

Holy Trinity Soup

Make this cleansing soup often and eat it a lot! Vary the vegetables but be sure to include the garlic, onion and ginger.

Serves 2

> *6 cloves garlic, left whole*
> *4 onions, halved*
> *1 inch of ginger root, left in one piece*
> *1 bay leaf*
> *1 quart spring water*
> *1 cup celery, sliced on the diagonal*
> *1 cup carrots, sliced on the diagonal*
> *2 unpeeled potatoes, cut into chunks*
> *1 cup asparagus, sliced on the diagonal*

Put garlic, onions, ginger root, bay leaf and spring water into a soup pot. Bring to a boil, reduce heat, and let simmer 2 hours. Remove garlic, onions and ginger root. Discard the ginger root.* Put the garlic and onion into a blender or food processor along with 1 ladle soup stock; puree. Pour pureed garlic and onion into the soup stock. Add the celery, carrots, potatoes and asparagus. Simmer 30 minutes longer, or until the vegetables are tender. Leftover rice and pieces of chicken can be added to make this soup an entire meal.

*If you enjoy hot spicy food with a strong ginger flavor, try leaving the ginger in with the onion and garlic while pureeing.

The Viscardis' Italian Bean Soup

Serves 4

15 ounces kidney beans, fresh or canned
5 cups water or soup stock (see page 92)
2 cloves fresh garlic, minced, or 1 teaspoon bottled minced garlic
15-ounce can garbanzo beans (also called chick-peas)
1 onion, chopped
2 carrots, chopped
2 stalks celery, chopped
¾ cup elbow macaroni
1 cup tomato sauce
2 tablespoons chopped fresh parsley
Freshly ground black pepper

Soak fresh beans overnight in enough water to cover them. The next day drain well. (Canned beans do not have to be soaked, but should be drained.)

Place the water or soup stock, drained kidney beans and garlic in a large soup pot. Bring mixture to a boil. If using fresh beans reduce heat and simmer 1 hour, until they are almost tender. If canned beans are used add both the kidney and garbanzo beans, and simmer 30 minutes. Add vegetables, bring again to a boil, reduce heat, and simmer 15 minutes. Add macaroni, tomato sauce and parsley, and continue to cook 15–20 minutes longer, or until the macaroni is tender. Serve with yeast-free crackers, and top with freshly ground pepper.

Bouillabaisse

Serves 4

2 tablespoons oil
1 cup chopped onion
1 cup chopped celery
2 cloves garlic, minced
½ cup sliced carrots
1 small bulb fennel, sliced (optional)
4 small turnips, sliced
3 tomatoes, chopped
5 cups water
½ teaspoon sea salt
½ teaspoon thyme
Pinch saffron (optional)
¼ teaspoon crushed red pepper
1 bay leaf
2 pounds lean fish fillet, cut into chunks
1½–2 dozen clams or mussels, well scrubbed
Juice of 1 lemon, or to taste

Heat oil in skillet, add chopped onion, celery and garlic. Stir fry several minutes until golden. Add carrots, fennel and turnips; stir. Add tomatoes, water, salt, thyme, saffron, red pepper and bay leaf. Bring to boil. Simmer over low heat, covered, for about 20 minutes. Add fish, clams or mussels, and lemon juice. Cover, and simmer gently another 15 minutes, or until fish is done and clams or mussels have opened.

To serve, place several pieces of fish and clams in each bowl, along with some of the vegetables. Ladle hot broth over fish and vegetables.

Manhattan-style Clam Chowder

Serves 6

2 tablespoons olive oil
1 clove fresh garlic, minced, or 1 teaspoon bottled minced garlic
2 onions, chopped
1 green pepper, chopped
2 carrots, sliced
2 stalks celery, sliced
1 16-ounce can peeled, seeded and chopped tomatoes
1 16-ounce can whole tomatoes in puree, juice reserved
4 potatoes, diced
½ teaspoon salt
1 teaspoon freshly ground pepper
1 teaspoon tarragon
½ teaspoon oregano
½ teaspoon thyme
5 cups water or soup stock (see page 92)
1 quart shucked chowder clams and their juice

Heat oil in large soup pot. Add garlic, onions and green pepper. Stir fry 3 minutes. Add carrots, celery, tomatoes and their juices, potatoes, salt, pepper, tarragon, oregano and thyme. Add stock, and bring to a boil. Reduce heat, cover, and cook until potatoes are almost tender. Add clams and their juice. Cover and simmer 15 minutes longer.

Fresh Onion Soup

This is a light onion soup recipe that can be varied according to your taste and the time of year. In summer we like this soup with fresh herbs instead of dry. In winter we use the dried herbs and the bouillon cube for a heartier fare.

Serves 4

> 4 tablespoons olive oil
> 2 cloves fresh garlic, minced, or 1 teaspoon bottled minced garlic
> 2 large onions, sliced
> ¼ cup whole-wheat flour
> Salt and pepper to taste
> 5 cups boiling spring water
> 1 beef bouillon cube (optional—be sure to read labels!)
> ½ teaspoon dried oregano, or 1 teaspoon fresh
> ½ teaspoon dried rosemary, or 1 teaspoon fresh
> ¼ teaspoon dried thyme, or ½ teaspoon fresh
> 2 teaspoons Kitchen Bouquet

Heat oil in a large soup pot. Add garlic and onions, and sauté 5 minutes. Add flour, salt and pepper. Sauté 1 minute more. Pour boiling water into soup pot, stirring constantly until flour mixture is smooth. Add bouillon cube, if desired. Reduce heat, add herbs and Kitchen Bouquet, cover, and simmer 1 hour. Check seasoning; add more as needed. Enjoy!

Vegetable Millet Soup

Serves 6

2 tablespoons olive oil
2 cloves fresh garlic, minced, or 1 teaspoon bottled minced garlic
2 stalks celery, chopped
2 onions, chopped
2 carrots, chopped
1 cup millet
8 cups water or soup stock (see page 92)
Salt and pepper to taste
2 bay leaves
½ teaspoon basil
½ teaspoon oregano
½ teaspoon thyme

Heat oil in a large soup pot. Add garlic, celery, onions and carrots. Sauté 3–5 minutes. Add millet, water, salt, pepper, and herbs to pot. Bring to a boil. Reduce heat, cover, and simmer 1 hour.

Miso Soup

Serves 6

- 2 tablespoons linseed oil
- 2 carrots, thinly sliced
- 2 stalks celery, thinly sliced
- 2 cloves fresh garlic, minced, or 1 teaspoon bottled minced garlic
- 1 onion, chopped
- ¼ head cabbage, cut into 1–2 inch strips
- 6 cups water or soup stock, (see page 92)
- 4 tablespoons miso paste (ask for miso at your natural-food store)

Heat oil in a large soup pot. Add carrots, celery, garlic, onion and cabbage. Stir fry 10 minutes. Add soup stock, bring to a boil. Reduce heat, cover, and simmer 20 minutes. Remove 1 ladle of stock and add miso paste to it. Stir until dissolved. Return to soup, and stir. Cover pot and remove from heat. Let sit for 5 minutes, then serve.

Split Pea Soup

Serves 6

1 tablespoon olive oil
1 onion, chopped
1 clove fresh garlic, minced, or 1 teaspoon bottled minced garlic
1 teaspoon ground cumin
2 cups uncooked split peas
2 quarts water
2 carrots, sliced
2 stalks celery, chopped
1 unpeeled potato, diced
Salt and pepper to taste

Heat oil in a large soup pot. Add onion, garlic, cumin. Sauté 1 minute. Add peas, and stir until coated. Add water, bring to a boil, reduce heat. Cover, and simmer 1 hour. Add remaining ingredients, and continue cooking 20–30 minutes, or until vegetables are tender. This soup really thickens overnight in the refrigerator. The taste is enhanced as well.

Chicken Barley Soup

Serves 6

Chicken parts (backs, necks—whatever)
Spring water
2 bay leaves
Pinch basil
1 clove garlic, minced
2 tablespoons chopped fresh parsley
4–5 scallions, chopped
½ pound snow peas
5 carrots, chopped
2 stalks celery, chopped
Pinches of thyme, oregano, salt and pepper
2 tomatoes, chopped
½ cup barley

Place chicken in soup pot. Fill ¾ full with water. Add bay leaves, basil, garlic and parsley. Cover, bring to a boil, and simmer 1 hour. Meanwhile, prepare vegetables. Set aside.

When chicken is tender, remove from pot, let cool and remove meat from bones. Place meat back into soup pot. Add remaining ingredients, and simmer as long as possible, at least 1 hour.

10
Recipes for a Yeast-free Dinner

Shrimp in Almond Sauce

Serves 2–4

3 tablespoons margarine
¾ cup slivered almonds, toasted
1 teaspoon poppy seeds
½ teaspoon garlic powder
1 pound small shrimp, peeled and cleaned

Melt margarine in a wok or large skillet. Add almonds, poppy seeds, garlic powder and shrimp. Stir fry 3–4 minutes, or until shrimp turn pink. Serve hot.

Chestnut Stuffing

Yields about 4 cups

3 tablespoons olive oil
2 onions, minced
2 cloves fresh garlic, minced, or 1 teaspoon bottled minced garlic
1 cup minced celery
1 tablespoon minced turnip
2 cups finely chopped chestnuts
½ cup crumbled stale yeast-free bread
1 teaspoon basil
1 teaspoon thyme
Freshly ground pepper to taste

Heat oil in wok or large skillet, add onions, garlic, celery and turnip. Stir fry 2 minutes. Add remaining ingredients, and heat through. Stuff into cavity of a turkey or chicken.

Shrimp-Stuffed Artichokes

Serves 4

4 artichokes
2 tablespoons olive oil
3 tablespoons minced onions
1 tablespoon minced garlic
1 teaspoon minced ginger
1 pound small, uncooked shrimp, peeled
Freshly ground pepper to taste
¼ teaspoon cayenne pepper

Prepare artichokes to be stuffed by first clipping the ends off all the leaves. Cut off the stems, so that the artichokes will stand upright. Spread the leaves apart as much as you can, running tap water over the artichoke as you're doing this. When the artichoke is open, pull out the center leaves and spoon out the section of fuzz. This can be discarded. The heart of the artichoke is found under the fuzz; this should be left intact. Place artichokes in a large pot or Dutch oven on a steamer rack over boiling water. Cover and steam 45–60 minutes, depending on size.

Meanwhile, place oil in a wok or large skillet; add onions, garlic, ginger, and sauté 1 minute. Add the shrimp, pepper and cayenne, and sauté 2–3 minutes, or until shrimp is pink. When artichokes are cooked, remove from pot, and drain by inverting. Then stuff shrimp mixture into the center of each artichoke. Serve immediately with tahini dip (see page 81).

Stuffed Manicotti

Serves 4

10 manicotti noodles
1 bunch broccoli
2 eggs
1 tablespoon olive oil
2 cloves fresh garlic, minced, or 1 teaspoon bottled minced garlic
1 tablespoon onion, minced
1 teaspoon oregano
1 teaspoon basil
½ teaspoon thyme
¼ teaspoon freshly ground pepper
2 cups tomato sauce (bottled or homemade, see page 127)

Preheat oven to 350° F. Prepare manicotti as directed on package. Meanwhile, finely chop broccoli; set aside. Beat eggs slightly in a small bowl. Heat oil in a wok or skillet, add garlic and onion; stir fry 1 minute. Add broccoli, and sauté 3 minutes. Stir in eggs, and continue to cook until egg is set. Mix oregano, basil, thyme, and pepper into the tomato sauce. Pour ½ of the sauce into the egg and broccoli mixture, and stir until blended. Stuff manicotti with broccoli mixture, pour ½ of the remaining tomato sauce in the bottom of a square baking dish. Place stuffed manicotti in baking dish, and cover with remaining sauce. Bake in oven for 20–30 minutes, or until heated through.

Chicken Supreme

Serves 4

4 boneless chicken breasts
½ pound fresh spinach
⅓ cup slivered raw almonds, toasted
2 cloves fresh garlic, minced, or 1½ teaspoons bottled minced garlic
4 teaspoons finely minced onion
1 tablespoon linseed oil
½ teaspoon oregano
½ teaspoon salt
2 cups uncooked brown rice
4½ cups water, or soup stock (for extra flavor—see page 92)
Freshly ground pepper to taste
2 tablespoons chopped fresh parsley

Preheat oven to 350° F. Remove skin from chicken breasts. Wash spinach, remove stems and discard, tear leaves into small pieces. Mix spinach and nuts together. In wok or large skillet, stir fry the garlic and 2 teaspoons of the minced onion in the oil. Add spinach, nuts, oregano and salt, and sauté 2–3 minutes longer. Remove from heat and let cool.

In a 10 x 13-inch baking dish, place uncooked rice and water or soup stock. Season with pepper, add remaining minced onion, and parsley. Set aside. Spread chicken breasts out flat. Pound lightly. Fill each with an equal portion of spinach mixture. Roll up and secure ends with toothpicks. Place rolls evenly over rice in baking dish. Cover with foil. Cook in oven for 1 hour and 15 minutes, or until rice is done.

Laura's Eggplant Pizza

This is an absolute *must* to try....

Serves 4

- 3 cups grated eggplant
- 3 eggs, beaten
- 1½ cups whole-wheat flour
- ¼ cup wheat germ
- 1 16-ounce can stewed tomatoes
- 1 12-ounce can tomato sauce
- ¼ teaspoon freshly ground pepper
- 1 teaspoon basil
- ½ teaspoon oregano
- 2 tablespoons olive oil
- 2 cloves garlic, minced
- 1 medium onion, chopped
- 2 bell peppers, chopped
- ½ small head cauliflower, thinly sliced
- 1 spear broccoli, thinly sliced

Preheat oven to 400° F. Mix eggplant, eggs, flour and wheat germ together. Spread onto a greased pizza pan. Bake in oven for 20 minutes, or until crust is lightly browned.

Meanwhile, in a large mixing bowl combine stewed tomatoes, tomato sauce, ground pepper, basil and oregano. Set aside. Heat oil in a wok or large skillet, add garlic, onion, bell peppers, cauliflower and broccoli. Stir fry 5–10 minutes.

When crust is done reduce oven heat to 350° F. Cover crust with tomato sauce, then layer with vegetable mixture, and cook pizza 30 minutes. Serve.

RECIPES FOR A YEAST-FREE DINNER

Millet and Vegetables

Millet is a staple of the Middle East. The light, crunchy texture and delicious flavor of this grain lends itself to breakfast cereals, as well as dinner casseroles. It's a cleansing grain and can be eaten often.

Serves 2

1 cup hulled millet
2 cups water or vegetable stock
1 cup snow peas
½ head cauliflower, chunked
2 spears broccoli, sliced
10–15 pearl onions
1 tablespoon olive oil
½ teaspoon each fresh oregano, basil and thyme
Freshly ground pepper to taste

Place millet in pot, cover with water or stock. Bring to boil, then simmer 25 minutes. Set aside and keep warm. Place peas, cauliflower, broccoli and onions on a steamer rack over boiling water. Cover, and steam until the vegetables are tender.

Meanwhile, in a large bowl, combine oil, fresh herbs and pepper. When vegetables are done, place in bowl with oil, and toss to coat all vegetables with oil and herbs. Place an equal portion of vegetables in the center of each individual serving plate. Put the millet around the border of the plate, circling the vegetables. Serve immediately.

Vegetarian Stuffed Bell Peppers

Serves 4

4 peppers
1 tablespoon olive oil
1 small onion, chopped
1 clove garlic, minced
1 teaspoon oregano
1 teaspoon basil
2 carrots, julienned or sliced extra thin on the diagonal
1 cup peas, fresh or frozen
1 tomato, diced
½ cup finely chopped walnuts
1½ cups cooked brown rice (see page 52)
2–3 cups tomato sauce, bottled or your favorite homemade (see page 127)

Preheat oven to 350° F. Wash and clean peppers. Cut off tops and remove seeds and membrane. Place prepared peppers on steamer rack in wok or Dutch oven, and steam 3–4 minutes.

Meanwhile, heat oil in wok or large skillet, add onion and garlic; sauté 1 minute. Add herbs, carrots and peas. Continue to cook 3–5 minutes, or until carrots are tender, stirring constantly. Reduce heat and add the tomato, walnuts, brown rice and ½ cup tomato sauce. Heat through. Stuff mixture into peppers. Spread ½ cup sauce in bottom of the baking dish. Stand peppers upright. Pour remaining sauce over the tops of peppers. Bake in oven for 30 minutes. Serve.

Pasta with Fresh Herbs

Serves 2

1 16-ounce package spinach or whole-wheat spaghetti
2 cloves fresh garlic minced, or 1½ teaspoons bottled minced garlic
3 tablespoons olive oil
2 tablespoons finely minced fresh parsley
2 tablespoons minced chives
1 teaspoon basil
½ teaspoon rosemary
½ teaspoon oregano

Prepare pasta as directed on package. Meanwhile, in skillet, sauté the garlic in the oil for 2 minutes. Pour the garlic, oil and herbs into a large bowl. When pasta is done, drain *well,* then place in the bowl with the garlic, herbs and oil. Toss until every piece of pasta glistens with oil. Serve and enjoy!

Baked Vegetable Pasta

Serves 4

1 pound package mostaccioli or ziti
1 tablespoon olive oil
2 cloves fresh garlic, minced, or 1 teaspoon bottled minced garlic
1 medium onion, finely minced
4 carrots, finely minced
2 cups broccoli, cut in small pieces
1½ teaspoons oregano
1 teaspoon basil
1 32-ounce bottle tomato sauce, or favorite homemade (see page 127)

Preheat oven to 350° F. Prepare pasta as directed on package. Drain well. Heat oil in wok or large skillet, add garlic and onion, stir fry 1 minute, and add carrots, broccoli, oregano and basil. Spread ½ cup tomato sauce in bottom of 10 x 13-inch baking dish. Layer pasta, vegetable mixture and tomato sauce. Top off with any remaining tomato sauce. Place in oven, and bake for 20 minutes, or until heated through. Serve.

RECIPES FOR A YEAST-FREE DINNER

Roasted Garlic Chicken with Crushed Herbs

Serves 4

1 whole chicken
¾ teaspoon fresh rosemary
½ teaspoon each basil and thyme
1 teaspoon minced fresh parsley
6 cloves garlic, peeled
1 lemon, cut in half and pierced with fork.

Preheat oven to 350° F. Clean and wash cavity of chicken. Place in roasting pan. Sprinkle cavity with half of each of the herbs. Stuff the chicken with 4 whole garlic cloves and the lemon wedges. Halve 1 garlic clove, and slip one half between each wing and the breast of the chicken. Sliver the last garlic clove, make slits in the chicken skin, and slip pieces of garlic between the skin and the meat. Sprinkle the remaining herbs on the top of the chicken. Cover with foil, and place in oven. Bake 1 hour, or until chicken is completely cooked. Remove foil for last 15 minutes of cooking to allow chicken to brown. Serve.

Steamed Fish with Chestnut Sauce

Serves 4

½ pound fresh chestnuts, or 1 5-ounce can whole chestnuts
Boiling water for cooking
1 stalk celery, finely chopped
1½ cups water
1 bay leaf
1 teaspoon sweet basil
Freshly ground pepper to taste
4 fish fillets (shark and halibut are especially good for this recipe)

To peel fresh chestnuts, drop into boiling water for 8 minutes. Turn the heat off, and while water is still hot, remove a few chestnuts at a time and peel. Place chestnuts and chopped celery in pot. Cover with 1½ cups water (if using canned chestnuts, include the water in which they are packed). Add bay leaf, basil and pepper; simmer over low heat for 1 hour. Meanwhile, prepare fish for steaming. In a large pot, place fish fillets on a steamer rack over boiling water. Cover pot securely, and steam 5–7 minutes, or until the fish flakes easily with a fork. Set aside and keep warm in the oven.

When chestnuts are done, remove bay leaf and discard. Place the chestnut mixture into a food processor or blender, and process until smooth. Spread over hot steamed fish. Serve.

Ginger Lobster Sauté

Serves 4

2 tablespoons oil
3 cups raw lobster meat
2 slices ginger root, minced
1 large zucchini, sliced diagonally
½ cup raw cashews
3 scallions, chopped
1½ cups broccoli, cut finely
4 cups hot cooked brown rice (see page 52)

Heat oil in skillet. Add lobster pieces and ginger; stir fry 2–3 minutes, or until lobster is white and firm. Remove to plate. Add zucchini, cashews, scallions and broccoli to skillet. Stir fry until tender. Return lobster to skillet, heat through. Serve immediately over brown rice.

Tarragon Chicken

Serves 4

2 tablespoons olive oil
2 pounds boneless chicken breast, diced
½ teaspoon dried tarragon
½ cup walnuts
2 scallions, chopped
2 carrots, finely sliced
Cooked brown rice (see page 52)

Heat oil in skillet. Stir fry chicken along with tarragon and walnuts until chicken is white. Remove to plate. Add scallions and carrots to skillet. Stir fry until tender crisp. Add chicken mixture to vegetables in skillet. Stir together. Serve hot over brown rice.

Savory Stuffed Cabbage

Serves 6

12 large cabbage leaves
6 tablespoons butter
1 large onion, finely chopped
1 carrot, finely chopped
½ bunch fresh parsley, minced
1 clove fresh garlic, minced, or ½ teaspoon bottled minced garlic
1½ pounds lean ground beef
1 cup cooked brown rice (see page 52)
1 egg, slightly beaten
Salt and pepper to taste
1 teaspoon basil
¼ teaspoon savory
¼ teaspoon thyme

Fill a large pot ¾ full with water, bring to a boil. Drop whole cabbage into pot, and blanch cabbage leaves in boiling water for 2–3 minutes. Drain cabbage. Pull off 12 outer leaves; set aside. Heat 2 tablespoons butter in skillet, add onion, carrot, parsley and garlic; sauté 3–5 minutes. Remove to large bowl. Add meat and rice to bowl, and mix well. Add remaining ingredients and mix again.

Flatten cabbage leaves. Place portion of meat mixture on each leaf and roll up, tucking in ends to seal; secure with toothpicks or string. Heat the remaining 4 tablespoons butter in large skillet, and gently sauté the cabbage rolls until lightly browned (3–4 minutes). It may be necessary to use two skillets to hold all the rolls. Reduce heat to low, cover, and cook 30 minutes, turning occasionally. Serve hot.

Steamed Sole with Almond Sauce

Serves 2

Sauce:
¾ cup butter
¾ cup slivered almonds, toasted
1 teaspoon poppy seeds

1 pound sole fillets
Juice of ½ lemon
3 sprigs fresh parsley

Prepare sauce. Melt butter in saucepan. Add almonds and poppy seeds. Stir fry 1 minute. Set aside. Place fish on greased heatproof platter, sprinkle with lemon juice and brush with almond sauce. Place parsley sprigs on top of fish. Fill large pot or Dutch oven with water, and bring to a boil. Place heatproof platter on steamer rack in pot. Cover. Steam 10 minutes, or until fish flakes easily with a fork. Serve.

YEAST-FREE LIVING

Trudy's Eggplant Experience

Many people shy away from eggplant because they are unsure of what to do with it. It has a terrific flavor and is low in calories. It can be prepared so many delicious ways; this is just one.

Serves 4

>1 tablespoon linseed oil
>1 tablespoon olive oil
>2 cloves fresh garlic, minced, or 1 teaspoon bottled minced garlic
>3 tablespoons minced onion
>1 cup diced eggplant
>½ cup chopped Brazil nuts
>1½ cups shrimp, shelled and cleaned
>2 cups cooked brown rice (see page 52)

Heat oils in a large skillet, add garlic and onion, and stir fry 2 minutes. Add eggplant, nuts and shrimp; continue to cook 3–5 minutes longer. Add cooked brown rice, and heat through.

Imambaldi

Our friend Russell Bennett created this recipe as his interpretation of this popular Middle Eastern dish, and we have adapted his recipe to fit in with the yeast-free living diet.

Imambaldi has a legend to go along with its exotic flavor. A sultan invited a priest to dinner, but neglected to tell his wife. She scurried into the kitchen on the guest's arrival, and blended all her leftovers together to create a dish that the priest loved. They drank and ate for hours. Then, to the hosts' surprise, the priest fainted! Hence the name "Imambaldi," which translates to "the priest has fainted." When he revived, he sputtered that the reason he had fainted was that he was overwhelmed with how wonderful the dinner had been!

Serves 4–6

2 large eggplants
½ cup olive oil
1 large onion, chopped
1 clove fresh garlic, minced, or ½ teaspoon bottled minced garlic
2 tablespoons minced fresh parsley
1 large tomato, chopped
1 tablespoon curry powder
¼ teaspoon freshly ground pepper

Preheat oven to 375° F. Cut eggplant into 2-inch-thick rounds (about 3 to an eggplant). Scoop out pulp (reserve), leaving a ⅔-inch-thick cuplike shell. Set aside. Finely chop eggplant pulp. Set aside. Heat 2 tablespoons of the oil in a large skillet. Add onion and garlic, and stir fry 2 minutes. Add chopped eggplant, parsley, tomato, curry powder and pepper. Stir fry 3 minutes. Remove from heat. Place remaining oil in a large baking pan. With your fingers, rub oil over each eggplant cup. Place cups face up in the baking pan. Fill cups with chopped eggplant mixture. Cover pan with foil. Bake in oven 30 minutes, covered, then 15 minutes, uncovered. Remove from oven, pour off excess oil, and let cool. Can be served warm or cold.

Maria's Meat Tamales

This recipe comes from the kitchen of Maria Arrizon. She is a wonderful cook and has a personality to match! She has given us many Mexican recipes and has filled our tummies with fabulous food. This recipe makes the perfect amount for hungry guests at a Mexican fiesta. But don't worry—if you don't have an army to feed, these tamales freeze well. We are sure you will enjoy them!

Yields 60–65 tamales

Meat filling:
- 6½ pounds meat (chicken, beef or pork)
- 1½ cups water
- 1 3-ounce package of chili pasilla
- 3 cloves fresh garlic, minced, or 1½ teaspoons bottled minced garlic
- Salt to taste

Place meat and 1 cup water in a 5-quart pot, bring to a boil, and cook meat until tender. Drain and reserve the broth for dough. Cool meat and shred. Meanwhile, boil chili pasilla in ½ cup water for 30 minutes. When done, carefully remove seeds and discard. Place chili, water in which it was cooked, and garlic in a blender. Blend 2 minutes. In a pan, mix chili mixture with shredded meat and salt. Stir fry mixture 3 minutes; set aside.

Dough:
- 10 pounds corn dough (masa harina—bought at your local Mexican food store)
- 2 pounds lard, melted
- 6 tablespoons baking powder
- Salt to taste
- 4 tablespoons red chili powder

> ½ cup reserved broth, or more if necessary to make dough moist and spreadable
>
> 2–3 packages corn husks (can be found in most grocery stores)

Place dough in a large bowl. Make a medium-sized hole in the center of the dough. Place lard, baking powder, salt, chili powder and broth in hole. Beat well until the dough mixture is a moist, spreading consistency. Place 2½ large spoonfuls of dough mixture on each corn husk, spreading evenly. Place about 3 tablespoons of meat filling on the dough. Roll husk up lengthwise, and fold in half. Place folded tamales on steamer rack over boiling water; cover. Cook over medium heat for 1½ hours, or until done. Serve.

Maria's Mole de Gallina

This dish provided by Maria Arrizon is usually made with chocolate, but to fit the yeast-free diet we switched to carob. We are happy to say that it is still *delicious!*

Serves 6

> 1 chicken, cut into pieces
> 3 cups water
> 1 3-ounce package of chili pasilla (can be found in most grocery stores; if not check your local Mexican food store, or food catalogues)
> 3 cloves fresh garlic, minced, or 1½ teaspoons bottled minced garlic
> 1 tablespoon carob
> 3 tablespoons oil
> 2 tablespoons flour
> Salt to taste

In a 3-quart pot, place chicken and 2 cups of the water; bring to a boil, and cook until tender. Drain off broth and reserve.

Place the chili pasilla and 1 cup water in a pot, and bring to a boil; reduce heat, cover, and simmer for 30 minutes. When done, remove seeds and discard. Reserve water. Place chili, garlic, carob and water chili was cooked in into a blender. Blend for 2 minutes.

In a large skillet, heat oil and flour together; cook until golden. Pour in chili mixture, little by little, stirring constantly. If necessary, add water to reserved chicken broth to make 3 cups. Slowly add to skillet, stirring constantly. Add salt, and bring to a boil. Add chicken pieces, bring to a boil again. Serve immediately and enjoy!

RECIPES FOR A YEAST-FREE DINNER

Lobster Linguine

Serves 4

1 16-ounce package linguine
2 tablespoons olive oil
1 clove fresh garlic, minced, or 1 teaspoon bottled minced garlic
2 scallions, minced
½ teaspoon oregano
½ teaspoon basil
½ teaspoon paprika
8 ounces lobster meat, canned, fresh, or frozen
32 ounces tomato sauce, canned or homemade (see page 127)

Prepare linguine as directed on package. Drain well. Meanwhile, heat oil in a wok or large skillet. Add garlic, scallions, oregano, basil, paprika and lobster meat. Sauté 3 minutes. Add tomato sauce, and heat through. Pour over linguine, toss well and serve.

Vegetable/Seafood Tempura

Choose vegetables, fish and seafood from list below. Recipe makes enough batter to coat tempura for 4.

Variety of vegetables and seafood:
Cauliflower, cut into small flowerets
Broccoli, cut into small flowerets
Fresh snap beans, cut into 2–3-inch pieces
Onion, cut into thick rings
Zucchini, sliced lengthwise into 2–3-inch strips
Bell pepper, cut into thick rings
Halibut fish fillets, cut into 2-inch chunks
Shrimp, shelled and cleaned
Scallops, cleaned

Tempura batter:
Peanut oil for deep frying
2 eggs
1 cup minus 1 tablespoon ice water
¾ cup unbleached flour
½ teaspoon salt

Heat a wok or deep frying pan. Fill ⅔ full with oil. It's ready at 375° F. Beat the eggs with the ice water. Add the flour and salt, and beat very lightly. The secret of tempura is very hot oil and very cold batter. Fill a large bowl with ice cubes and cold water and set the batter bowl in it.

Dip sliced vegetables and seafood in batter, and carefully drop into hot oil. Start with 1 or 2 pieces; as the oil gets very hot, more can be cooked at once. When they bounce up to the surface and are golden, they're ready. Drain on paper towels. Keep the finished tempura in a warm oven until ready to serve.

RECIPES FOR A YEAST-FREE DINNER

My Mama's Truly Italian Spaghetti Sauce

This is Mama Viscardi's famous sauce recipe, adapted for yeast-free living!

> 1 large can (2 pounds 3 ounces) peeled Italian plum tomatoes (with basil if possible)
> Olive oil for cooking
> 1 clove fresh garlic, minced, or 1 teaspoon bottled minced garlic
> 1 small onion, chopped
> 1 small can tomato paste
> 1 can water
> ½ teaspoon salt
> 1 basil leaf
> ¼ teaspoon oregano
> Pasta

Puree tomatoes in blender for 1 second, or go through and remove stems and cores by hand. Set aside. Heat oil in a large pot. Add garlic and onion. Stir fry 3 minutes. Pour in tomatoes, and simmer. Add tomato paste and 1 can water, stir, simmer 15 minutes. Add salt, basil leaf and oregano, stir, and simmer at least 30 minutes. The longer it simmers the better it tastes!

Prepare pasta according to directions on package. (To judge amounts, figure 1 pound of pasta for 4 people.) Drain well, toss with sauce. Serve.

Fettuccine with Tuna Sauce

Serves 4

1 16-ounce package fettuccine
1 can tuna, drained
1 tablespoon sesame seeds
3 cups tomato sauce
½ teaspoon oregano
½ teaspoon basil
¼ teaspoon garlic powder
2 tablespoons minced fresh parsley

Prepare fettuccine as directed on package. Drain well. Meanwhile, heat all other ingredients in a saucepan until heated through. When fettuccine is done, pour sauce over top. Serve with a fresh green salad.

RECIPES FOR A YEAST-FREE DINNER

Conchiglie with Clam Sauce

Conchiglie (seashell-shaped pasta) is excellent when you don't want to leave even a single drop of sauce on your plate. With sauce like this, we can guarantee you'll want to use conchiglie!

Serves 4

1 16-ounce package conchiglie
2 dozen clams
1 tablespoon linseed oil
2 tablespoons finely minced onion
3 cloves fresh garlic, minced, or 2 teaspoons bottled minced garlic
16-ounce bottle tomato sauce, or your favorite homemade (see page 127)
$1/2$ teaspoon oregano
$1/2$ teaspoon basil
$1/8$ teaspoon salt
$1/2$ teaspoon freshly ground pepper

Prepare pasta as directed on package. Drain well. Meanwhile, scrub clams and place on a steamer rack over boiling water; steam just until the shells open. Reserve 8 clams in shells for garnish. Cut remaining clams loose from shells.

Heat oil in a wok or large skillet. Add onion and garlic, and sauté 3 minutes. Add remaining ingredients along with clams, and heat through. Pour clam sauce over hot pasta, and toss. Garnish each plate with 2 clams in shell; serve.

Italian Zucchini Stew

Serves 6

8 potatoes, washed and diced
6 zucchini, chopped into chunks
1 large or 2 small onions, sliced
10 brussels sprouts, halved
1 small bunch fresh parsley, minced
2 carrots, cut into chunks
2 cloves fresh garlic, minced, or 1 teaspoon bottled minced garlic
2 16-ounce bottles tomato sauce, or your favorite homemade (see page 127)
Freshly ground pepper

Prepare all vegetables and place in a large soup pot. Add tomato sauce, bring to a boil, cover, and cook 30–40 minutes, or until potatoes are tender. Top with freshly ground pepper. Serve hot with your favorite yeast-free crackers.

Shrimp Creole

We've had the pleasure of eating authentic southern Louisiana shrimp creole. Unfortunately this has spoiled us: now we only want the best. This recipe comes as close as you can get without having to fly to New Orleans.

Serves 8

1 onion, chopped
½ cup chopped green pepper
¼ cup chopped celery
2 cloves garlic, minced
5 tablespoons oil
2 8-ounce cans tomato sauce (read labels), or your favorite homemade (see page 127)
3 pounds raw shrimp, peeled
1 tablespoon chopped parsley
Salt and pepper to taste
Cayenne pepper to taste
Hot cooked brown rice (see page 52)

In a large pot, sauté onion, green pepper, celery and garlic in oil until onion is transparent. Add tomato sauce, and bring to a boil; reduce heat and simmer, uncovered, 40 minutes. Add shrimp and remaining ingredients, except rice, and cook 15 minutes longer, or until thick. Serve over hot cooked rice.

11

Recipes for Yeast-free Breads and Spreads

In the original outline of this book, we didn't include a bread recipe section. We thought that finding yeast-free bread would be easy for our readers. However, after searching the shelves of natural-food stores and finding few selections, and experimenting with familiar yeast-free recipes—we found the breads to be dry, dense and generally unacceptable—our imaginations were aroused, and we set about to create a chapter of yeast-free recipes that would be truly enjoyable. It wasn't easy—without sugar and yeast, bread is not quite the same. After many hours of testing we are proud to present the following collection of interesting and delicious, sugar- and yeast-free, breads.

Whole-wheat Irish Soda Bread

This nontraditional soda bread recipe will surprise and delight you. The texture is light and moist, and the flavor is sensational.

Yields 1 loaf

2½ cups whole-wheat flour
1½ teaspoons baking soda
½ teaspoon salt
1 cup low-fat milk
¼ cup water

Preheat oven to 400° F. Combine flour, soda and salt. Add milk and half the water. Stir until dry ingredients are just moistened. Add more water, as necessary, to make a soft dough. Place dough on a lightly floured surface. Knead briefly, shape into a round loaf. Put on a lightly greased baking sheet. Cut a bold cross on top; extend cuts over the sides so the bread will not crack while baking. Bake in oven 25–30 minutes, or until bread is golden.

Tip to test for doneness: Remove bread from sheet and tap on the bottom. If the bread sounds hollow, it's done. If not, return to baking sheet and continue to cook.

Rye Rolls

These are a perfect accompaniment to a hearty bowl of soup on a cool day.

Yields 12

1⅛ cups rye flour
1 cup yellow cornmeal
1 cup whole-wheat flour
2 teaspoons baking soda
1 teaspoon salt
1 large egg, slightly beaten
⅔ cup plain yogurt
⅓ cup water

Preheat oven to 375° F. In a large bowl, combine 1 cup of the rye flour along with the remaining dry ingredients; set aside. In a separate bowl, combine egg, yogurt and water. Add liquid ingredients to flour mixture, and stir until a soft dough forms. Turn dough out onto a lightly floured surface, and knead briefly, adding the remaining ⅛ cup of rye flour as needed. Cut dough into 12 individual balls. Place each ball onto a lightly greased baking sheet. Cut a bold cross in the top of each ball. Bake in oven for 20 minutes, or until done.

YEAST-FREE LIVING

Almond Bread

This bread rises nicely. Its dense, almondy flavor is perfect at teatime.

Yields 1 loaf

> 2 cups whole-wheat flour
> ½ cup bran flakes
> ¼ teaspoon salt
> ½ teaspoon baking soda
> ½ teaspoon baking powder
> 2 eggs, slightly beaten
> ¼ cup water (or try substituting unsweetened apple juice for the water)
> ⅔ cup plain yogurt
> ½ cup low-fat milk
> 2 teaspoons almond extract
> ¾ cup finely chopped almonds

Preheat oven to 375° F. In a large bowl, combine flour, bran flakes, salt, soda and baking powder. In a separate bowl, combine eggs, water, yogurt, milk and almond extract; beat with a fork until smooth. Add the liquid ingredients to the flour mixture; stir. Stir in the nuts. Pour batter into a lightly greased loaf pan. Bake in oven for 40–50 minutes, or until done.

RECIPES FOR YEAST-FREE BREADS AND SPREADS

Quick Banana-Nut Bread

Yields 1 loaf

¼ *cup vegetable shortening*
1 teaspoon vanilla
3 eggs plus 1 tablespoon water
1¾ cups whole-wheat flour
2 teaspoons baking powder
¼ teaspoon salt
1 teaspoon baking soda
1 cup mashed ripe banana
½ cup chopped walnuts

Preheat oven to 375° F. Beat shortening, vanilla, eggs and water together until mixture is creamy. Combine dry ingredients in a large mixing bowl. Add liquid ingredients. Beat in banana until batter is smooth. Stir in nuts. Pour batter into a lightly greased loaf pan. Bake in oven for about 40–45 minutes, or until done. Cool completely before slicing.

Corn Bread

Serves 8–12

1½ cups yellow cornmeal
½ cup unbleached flour
2½ teaspoons baking powder
½ teaspoon salt
½ teaspoon baking soda
2 eggs, slightly beaten
½ cup plain yogurt
¼ cup water
½ onion, chopped
2 jalapeño peppers, finely chopped
½ cup fresh corn cut from cob

Preheat oven to 375° F. In a large mixing bowl, combine dry ingredients. In a separate bowl, combine the eggs, yogurt and water. Gradually add to dry ingredients, stirring just until moistened. Stir in onion, peppers and corn. Pour batter into a lightly greased square baking pan. Bake in oven for 35–45 minutes, or until done.

Orange-Walnut Bread

Yields 2 loaves

2 cups whole-wheat flour
1 cup unbleached flour
3 teaspoons baking powder
1 teaspoon baking soda
½ teaspoon cream of tartar
1 tablespoon grated orange peel
1 egg
½ cup fresh-squeezed orange juice
¾ cup low-fat milk
¼ cup water
½ cup walnuts
¼ cup linseed oil

Preheat oven to 350° F. In a large bowl, combine flours, baking powder, soda and cream of tartar. In a separate bowl, combine orange peel, egg, orange juice, milk, water, nuts and oil. Gradually pour liquid ingredients into dry ingredients. Stir just to moisten the dry ingredients. Pour batter into 2 lightly greased loaf pans. Bake in oven for 35–40 minutes, or until done.

Sesame/Poppy Crackers

Yields 2 dozen

1½ cups whole-wheat flour
¼ cup unbleached flour
¼ cup sesame seeds
3 teaspoons poppy seeds
½ teaspoon salt
⅓ cup oil
½ cup water

Preheat oven to 350° F. Stir flours, seeds and salt together. Add oil and water, and stir until mixed. Roll out dough to ⅛ inch thick, and cut into cracker shapes. Place on ungreased baking sheet. Bake in oven 15–20 minutes, or until crackers are crisp and golden.

Chapati

Yields 1

1 cup whole-wheat flour
1 cup cornmeal
½ teaspoon salt
Water

Mix dry ingredients together. Mix water into the flour mixture until the dough rolls away from the sides of the bowl, but does not become sticky. Flatten dough with your hands, and place chapati in an oiled skillet. Cook 10 minutes over medium heat. Flip, and cook an additional 10 minutes.

RECIPES FOR YEAST-FREE BREADS AND SPREADS

Chunky Apple-Banana Muffins

These muffins are moist and delicious; the chunked fruit lends an interesting texture.

Yields 12

- 1 cup whole-wheat flour
- 1 cup unbleached flour
- 3 teaspoons baking powder
- ¼ teaspoon salt
- 3 teaspoons cinnamon
- ½ teaspoon ginger
- ¼ teaspoon nutmeg
- 2 eggs
- ⅓ cup oil
- 1 cup unsweetened applesauce
- 1 apple, chopped
- 1 banana, diced

Preheat oven to 375° F. In a large bowl, combine flours, baking powder, salt and spices. In a separate bowl, combine eggs, oil and applesauce. Mix liquid ingredients with the flour mixture, and stir until blended. Add apple and banana chunks, and stir. Pour batter into greased muffin tins. Bake in oven for 30 minutes.

Breadsticks

Yields 15–20

2 cups whole-wheat flour
2 cups unbleached flour
1 teaspoon salt
2 tablespoons olive oil
2 cups water
Sesame seeds

Combine flours and salt together. Add oil and water, and mix together. Add more water if necessary, but dough should not get sticky. Let set 1 hour.

Preheat oven to 375° F. Shape dough into breadsticks ¾ inch x 6 inches long. Roll in sesame seeds. Bake in oven for 20 minutes, until slightly browned.

Popovers

Yields 6–8

1 cup whole-wheat flour (unbleached flour may be substituted)
½ teaspoon salt
3 eggs
½ cup low-fat milk
½ cup water
2 tablespoons olive oil

Preheat oven to 400° F. Combine flour and salt in a large bowl. Add eggs, milk, water and oil. Beat with an electric mixer just until smooth. Pour batter into greased custard cups, filling each about ½ full. Place on a baking sheet in oven and bake for 40–50 minutes, or until golden brown. Serve hot.

RECIPES FOR YEAST-FREE BREADS AND SPREADS

Brown-Rice Wheat Muffins

Yields 12

1½ cups whole-wheat flour
4 teaspoons baking powder
½ teaspoon salt
3 eggs
⅓ cup melted margarine
½ cup cooked brown rice
¼ cup shredded carrots

Preheat oven to 400° F. Combine flour, baking powder and salt together; set aside. Beat eggs and margarine together lightly. Add rice and carrots. Mix with dry ingredients, and stir just until moistened. Spoon into a greased muffin tin. Bake in oven for 20 minutes, or until lightly browned.

Apple Spread

Yields about 3 cups

6 apples, cored and thinly sliced
1 cup unsweetened apple juice
1½ teaspoons cinnamon
½ teaspoon nutmeg
½ teaspoon ground cloves

Combine all ingredients in a large saucepan. Bring to a boil. Reduce heat, cover, and simmer 20 minutes, or until apples are tender. Place in a blender, and blend until very smooth.

Apple Preserves

Yields about 2 cups

3 apples, peeled and cut into chunks*
¼ cup unsweetened apple juice
1½ tablespoons tapioca

Place apple chunks and juice into a saucepan, cover, and cook until apples are tender. Add tapioca, and bring to a boil, stirring constantly. Remove from heat, mash apples lightly with a wooden spoon, and cool thoroughly. Cover, and store in the refrigerator.

Raspberry Jam

Yields about 3 cups

16 ounces unsweetened raspberries, fresh or frozen†
¼ cup fresh-squeezed orange juice
1½ tablespoons tapioca

Combine all ingredients in a saucepan. Let sit 5 minutes. Bring to a boil over medium heat, stirring constantly. Simmer 2 minutes. Cool thoroughly. Cover, and store in refrigerator.

---

*Plums, peaches or nectarines may be substituted for the apples to make a variety of preserves.

†Unsweetened strawberries, blackberries or boysenberries may be substituted for the raspberries—or try mixing two different berries together.

12

Recipes for Yeast-free Desserts

Apple/Pear Delight

This dessert is so nutritious and delicious it can double as a light meal. We use it a lot for picnics and car trips.

Serves 4–6

> 4 apples
> 2 small pears
> 1 cup cooked millet
> 2 teaspoons cinnamon
> ½ teaspoon nutmeg
> ¼ cup chopped Brazil nuts
> Plain yogurt (optional)

Peel apples and pears, and cut into small chunks. Place pear and apple chunks on a steamer rack over boiling water. Cover and steam 10 minutes, or until tender.

Place pears and apples into a blender and whip until fairly smooth. Pour blended fruit into a large bowl, and stir in millet, spices and nuts. Pour into individual custard cups. Delicious warm or chilled. For a treat add a dollop of yogurt.

RECIPES FOR YEAST-FREE DESSERTS

Pastina Banana Splits

Serves 4

2 cups cooked pastina, cooled
1 cup sliced strawberries
1 cup seedless purple grapes
1 cup chunked fresh pineapple
1 cup yogurt, plain or vanilla flavored
4 small bananas, sliced in half lengthwise
Whole strawberries for garnish

Cook pastina according to directions on package. Drain well. In a large bowl, mix together cooked pastina, fruit, except bananas and whole strawberries, and yogurt. Refrigerate until thoroughly chilled. Place 2 slices of banana on each individual serving dish. Scoop equal portions of fruit mixture over bananas. Top each with a whole strawberry, and serve.

Layered Fresh Fruit, Gelatin and Yogurt

Serves 2–4

1 cup water
1 cup fresh-squeezed orange juice
1 envelope unflavored gelatin
1 cup sliced, unsweetened strawberries
¾ cup plain yogurt

Combine water, juice and gelatin in a saucepan. Bring mixture to a boil, stirring constantly. Stir until gelatin dissolves. Pour into a dish and chill until partially set. Layer the fruit, thickened gelatin and yogurt in individual parfait glasses. Refrigerate until completely set.

Brown Rice Pudding

Serves 4

2 eggs, lightly beaten
¾ cup water
1 teaspoon vanilla
1 teaspoon lemon juice
⅛ teaspoon salt
1 teaspoon cinnamon
¼ teaspoon nutmeg
⅛ teaspoon ginger
2 cups cooked brown rice
1 apple, finely chopped

Mix all ingredients together in saucepan. Cook over low heat until mixture is thickened and apples are tender; stir occasionally.

Chunky Applesauce

Serves 6

8 apples, chunked
2 bananas, sliced
1 cup water or unsweetened apple juice
1 teaspoon cinnamon
1 tablespoon wheat germ
¼ teaspoon nutmeg
⅓ cup chopped walnuts

Place apple chunks and banana slices in a pan along with the water or juice. Cook covered over low heat, stirring occasionally, until apples start to soften—about 10–15 minutes. Add cinnamon, wheat germ, nutmeg and nuts; stir to slightly mash apples. Cook uncovered 5 more minutes, stirring occasionally. Serve warm or cold.

Stuffed Apple Bowls

Serves 6

6 red apples
½ cup chopped raw cashews
½ cup fresh-squeezed orange juice
3 tablespoons melted margarine
¼ teaspoon nutmeg
¼ teaspoon ground cloves
½ teaspoon cinnamon
Plain yogurt (optional)

Preheat oven to 375° F. Prepare apples by cutting a small slice off the bottom of each apple to allow it to stand upright. Core, and make a shallow horizontal slit all around the outside of each apple; this will allow for expansion while cooking. Set apples in a shallow baking pan. Fill each apple with cashews. Mix orange juice, margarine, nutmeg, cloves and cinnamon together. Drizzle over apples. Bake in oven for 40 minutes. Serve with yogurt.

Cinnamon-Apple Pears

Serves 8

3 cups apple juice
8 black peppercorns
4 whole cloves
1 2-inch stick cinnamon
1 1-inch piece vanilla bean
4 pears

Place all ingredients, except pears, in wok or large saucepan. Bring to a boil over high heat; boil, uncovered, 3–4 minutes. Add pears and reduce heat. Simmer, uncovered, 15 minutes, or until pears are tender, but not mushy. Carefully, remove pears to a large bowl. Over high heat, boil the remaining liquid until it is reduced to 2 cups. Strain liquid over pears in bowl. Cool. Serve pear halves with liquid spooned over them.

Peach-Yogurt Freeze

Serves 4

2 cups plain yogurt
1/4 teaspoon cinnamon
1/8 teaspoon nutmeg
1/4 teaspoon salt
2 pounds fresh or frozen ripe peaches, finely diced

Place all ingredients, except peaches, in a blender. (An electric mixer may be used.) Blend until well combined. Add peaches and blend until smooth. Pour into an 8-inch-square pan or ice-cube trays. Place in freezer until almost frozen through.

Remove from freezer. Cut into small cubes, or remove from ice-cube trays. Place in a large chilled bowl. Beat until smooth, but not melted. Place in a large airtight container, and freeze until firm. Allow to soften slightly before serving.

Apple Fritters

Yields 25–30

1½ cups whole-wheat flour
Pinch salt
1½ teaspoons baking powder
½ teaspoon baking soda
4 apples
½ teaspoon cinnamon
½ teaspoon nutmeg
¼ teaspoon ground cloves
2 eggs
¼ cup plain yogurt
⅔ cup water
Peanut oil for deep frying

In a large bowl, combine flour, salt, baking powder and soda. Core and finely chop apples. Sprinkle apples with the cinnamon, nutmeg and cloves. Add apples to flour mixture, along with the eggs, yogurt and water. Mix to form batter. Heat wok or deep frying pan ⅔ full with peanut oil. Test temperature by placing 1 tablespoon of batter in hot oil. Oil should bubble, and fritter should quickly rise to surface.

Drop remaining batter by the tablespoonful into hot oil. Cook fritters until golden on both sides. Drain on paper towels. Serve hot.

13
Maintaining a Yeast-free Lifestyle

The time it takes to get well depends upon the severity of your yeast infection. Healing is a gradual process, but hopefully you will discover that your symptoms lessen and your strength and good health return. When this occurs it is most important *not* to return to old bad habits. It is best to consider yourself cured but susceptible to yeast infection.

The best maintenance method is to continue on the dietary cleansing program, but perhaps adhere to it less stringently. Allow yourself a little leeway—but remain *conscious* of the foods you ingest and your reaction to them. Your body will let you know. After the body is clean, it generally reacts negatively when such products as sugar, red meat and alcohol are ingested. Go slowly. Treat yourself delicately. Monitor your body's response. You have given yourself a new lease on life—*protect* it, *cherish* it and, most of all, be *moderate* in the use of products you know you should avoid. Keep taking your vitamins. Your maintenance program should include your vitamin and mineral supplement, including vitamins C and E and calcium, as described in Chapter 3. It is also important to stay away from antibiotics, birth-control pills, leftover foods, canned juices and products containing high concentrations of yeast. Try also to eliminate stress buildup.

It is also important to eliminate environmental yeast and mold. Damp basements and bathrooms are favorite places for yeast contamination. Keep them meticulously clean. Even wood can harbor bacteria and yeast. So, if you are in the market for a new bed, you might consider replacing wood with iron or brass. Also be sure that your kitchen is adequately ventilated and that the refrigerator is kept very clean. Avoid humidifiers, as they encourage mold. Get rid of decaying leaves and compost outside your home.

Most of all, remain *aware*. The following list of books, tapes and publications will help keep you informed about matters concerning your health. *Becoming* healthy is the first step, *staying* healthy is the second. Your efforts will be well rewarded, as a cared-for body is an energetic, comfortable, responsive vehicle for a happy, full life.

FOR FURTHER INFORMATION

Update, a quarterly periodical published by the Gesell Institution of Human Development. Send a stamped, self-addressed envelope to: Update, 310 Prospect Street, New Haven, CT 06511.

Crook, William, M.D. "Yeast Tapes." Send a stamped, self-addressed enveloped to: Yeast Information, Box 1000, Jackson, TN 38301.

FOR A MAINTENANCE FOOD PROGRAM

Annechild, Annette. *Getting Into Your Wok with Annette Annechild.* New York: Wallaby Books. Available at bookstores, or contact Simon & Schuster, 1230 Avenue of the Americas, New York, NY 10020.

———. *The Seafood Wok.* New York: Wallaby Books. Available at bookstores, or contact Simon & Schuster, 1230 Avenue of the Americas, New York, NY 10020.

———. *Wok Your Way Skinny.* New York: Wallaby Books. Available at bookstores, or contact: Simon & Schuster, 1230 Avenue of the Americas, New York, NY 10020.

Crook, William, M.D. *The Yeast Connection.* A comprehensive study of yeast infection. Available at bookstores, or contact: Professional Books, P.O. Box 3494, Jackson, TN 38301.

Truss, Orian, M.D. *The Missing Diagnosis.* Contact: P.O. Box 26508, Birmingham, AL 35226. The book costs $27.50 postpaid.